WAR DANCE

T0163520

War Dance

Plains Indian Musical Performance

William K. Powers

The University of Arizona Press
Tucson & London

The University of Arizona Press

Copyright © 1990
The Arizona Board of Regents
All Rights Reserved

This book was set in Linotron 202 Meridien.
⊗ This book is printed on acid-free, archival-quality paper.
Manufactured in the United States of America.

94 93 92   5 4 3 2

Library of Congress Cataloging-in-Publication Data

Powers, William K.
    War dance : Plains Indian musical performance / William K. Powers.
        p. cm.
    Includes bibliographical references.
    ISBN 0-8165-1170-5 (cloth); 0-8165-1365-1 (paper); alk. paper.
    1. Oglala Indians—Dance. 2. Oglala Indians—Music. 3. Indians
of North America—Great Plains—Dance. 4. Indians of North America—
Great Plains—Music. I. Title
    E99.O3P682   1990
    781.62'97301554-dc20   90-32421
                                                              CIP

British Library Cataloguing in Publication data are available.

Frontispiece: Mato Wamniomni (Whirlwind Bear).
Photo by E. A. Rinehart, Omaha, Nebraska, 1900.
Photo courtesy Museum für Volkerkunde, Vienna.

For David P. McAllester

Contents

Illustrations and Tables

Tables

Acknowledgments

A number of people have continued to lend encouragement to my work on music and dance. Foremost is my wife, Marla N. Powers, and my sons, Jeff and Greg. Marla continues to be my best critic, and in many ways each work of mine is a collaborative effort.

Next, of course, are all the singers and dancers whom I have met and performed with since 1948. In particular, all my ideas about music have been inspired initially by Henry White Calf, with whom I stayed at Loafer Camp; Edgar Red Cloud, of Pine Ridge; and William Horncloud, who in 1989 was 86 and still filled with enthusiasm for powwows and other Indian celebrations. My adopted father, Frank Afraid of Horse, remains my model of traditional Plains Indian dancing, and during his lifetime was considered one of the best by all who knew him.

Much of my time has been spent on the Pine Ridge reservation, where my adopted sisters, Zona Fills the Pipe and Sadie Janis, and my niece, Darlene (Janis) Shortbull, have made me and my family feel like part of theirs. The late Clarence Janis was in many ways my mentor, and he is sadly lost but happily remembered. In recent years, photographic and other archival materials have been made available through the kind offices of Reverend Earl Kurth, S.J., former President of the Heritage Center, Inc., and Reverend Peter Klink, S.J., Superior of Holy Rosary Mission, Pine Ridge, South Dakota. In particular, Brother C. M. Simon, S.J., Director of the Heritage Center, Inc., and the Red Cloud Indian Art Show at Holy Rosary, has made our stay each summer fruitful and entertaining. It would be difficult for me to name one other person who has been so dedicated and helpful to Indian artists, and to those of us who rely on his experience and knowledge of tribal arts to write about them.

Finally, it is with great pleasure that I humbly dedicate this volume to my friend, colleague, and teacher, David P. McAllester, Professor of Music and Anthropology Emeritus at Wesleyan University, Middletown, Connecticut. I first met Dave at the Society for Ethnomusicology meetings at Albuquerque, New Mexico, in 1965. He was particularly instrumental in helping me make up my mind to pursue an academic career in anthropology after having already spent 20 years singing and dancing Indian. He was also responsible for my subsequent attendance at Wesleyan, where I continued to sing and dance Indian for my room, board, and master's degree. His graciousness is matched only by that of his wife, Susan, who made all students at Wesleyan welcome, and I was lucky enough to be one of them. Most of all, I want to say that I regard Dave's attitude about life in general as admirable. He has a profound and loving respect for nature and people, and knows a lot about both. Although his own specialization has been with the Navajo, his philosophical ideas are steeped in cultural relativism tempered with an uncanny respect for that which is culturally similar as well as for that which is socially different. His ideas are applicable to all people who sing and dance. It has been a sincere pleasure to work and to be with him in the past, and he has my continued respect and profound admiration.

Introduction

The following essays represent my thoughts on Plains Indian music and dance over the past 30 years of publishing on the subject, particularly in the now defunct journal *American Indian Tradition*, and later in publications such as *Powwow Trails* and *American Indian Crafts and Culture*. More recently, most of my work has appeared in the *Journal of the Society for Ethnomusicology* and other academic journals.

My interest and involvement go back much further, to the time when I first encountered Lakota Indians from Pine Ridge, South Dakota, in my home town of St. Louis, Missouri. Like many other white boys of the time, I had already learned to perform what I perceived to be Indian dancing, beginning at age nine when I served as mascot for an Explorer Post called the Piasa Society. As was true with other such groups throughout the United States, there was not much expertise, but there was a great deal of enthusiasm. A number of academics began this way, and it is still a pleasure to meet someone at a conference whom I originally knew as an Indian dancer.

Anyway, it was 1947 when I accompanied my eighth-grade class from Scruggs School in South St. Louis to Keil Auditorium, the site of the International Folk Festival, which was headed by a dynamic woman named Sara Gertrude Knott, who was well known in folk-lore circles. Each year she directed and narrated the festival, which included the songs and dances of peoples from all over the world. Of particular interest to me was the fact that each year the festival opened with a selection of dances by American Indians. In the past, a group of Kiowas "held the contract," as they say in Indian country, to participate in the folk festival, but for some reason this year the singers and dancers were "Sioux" from Pine Ridge, South Dakota. This was particularly heartening to me because, like so many other young people of the time who read about Indians, the "Sioux" were my favorite but I never believed that I would be seeing them in person. That day I watched more eagerly and perhaps more nervously than ever before as the four Lakota men performed such dances as the Omaha dance, the Scalp dance, the Victory dance, and the Sacred Bow dance.

After the Indian part of the program concluded, I couldn't contain myself. Having been brought up in a theatrical family, I was very familiar with the numerous ways one could enter a theater, so I slipped away from my class and headed outside for the stage door. Apprehensive that the doorman would be reluctant to let a kid into the dressing room backstage area, I prepared myself and announced in a loud voice, "I want to see the Indians—please." Much to my relief, he rather nonchalantly, without looking up from his newspaper, said, "Second floor dressing rooms," and pointed the way over his shoulder.

When I got to the second floor, I could smell what I later discovered was *wahpe waštemna,* a sweet grass that the dancers used to pack with their costumes to keep them fresh. At the end of a concrete hallway there were dressing rooms and I could hear the men talking. I peeked into each of the rooms until I finally got to theirs. There they were:

John Colhoff, known as White Man Stands in Sight, was famous in his own right, having served as the public relations director for the Oglala Sioux Tribal Council and as summer curator of the Rapid City, South Dakota, Sioux Indian Museum. His name was listed frequently as a respondent for many western historians, particularly George E. Hyde of Omaha, Nebraska, who has written many wonderful histories of the Plains Indians.

Edgar Red Cloud, the singer for the group, was grandson of the famous old Chief Red Cloud of the Bad Face band of Oglalas. Later I would get to know Edgar very well, and he would be one of the first of the Lakotas to teach me how to sing and speak Lakota.

The other members of the groups were Joseph Elk Boy and Daniel White Eyes, who were old-timers whom I would never see again but whose families I would one day soon sing and dance with at Pine Ridge.

Self-consciously I said *"Hau Kola,"* one of ten expressions I had learned since first reading "Sioux" history in the third grade.

"Hau," they replied, somewhat surprised but nevertheless delighted upon hearing a gangling white boy who could at least say hello in their native language.

They made me feel at home immediately, just as they would at Pine Ridge in years to come. We talked about singing and dancing, and later I planned to come back every day as long as they were in town, which was an all-too-short five days. I did come back every day and relieved John of some of his chores. When the old-timers were too tired, for example, I would take them back to their hotel in downtown St. Louis by bus, being quite proud to walk next to what I assumed to be the tallest men I had ever seen, both of them with long hair and wearing moccasins with their street clothes.

Best of all during those five days was the invitation to come to Pine Ridge. Although my mother and father were somewhat concerned about their only son running away with the "wild" Indians, I made arrangements, at the advice of John, to contact the Jesuit Mission Bureau in St. Louis, which in turn put me in touch with the Reverend Leo Doyle, S.J., who was Superior at Holy Rosary Mission at Pine Ridge. Holy Rosary of course was well known to me. It was a focal point during the Wounded Knee Massacre in 1890, and many of the priests, brothers, and nuns had been mentioned in the history books for their efforts to make peace with Indians who had left Pine Ridge to go up to the Stronghold at Sheep Mountain in the Badlands.

After waiting what seemed to be an eternity for a response from Father Doyle, the letter came, and I was invited to come. The next summer, I went. And I have returned nearly every year since. Frequently I have made as many as four trips a year in order to conduct research that was in some way seasonal. Each year, I feel the same exhilaration I felt in 1948.

Since 1948, I have continued to go to dances that are now generally called powwows, but that at one time were referred to by tribal terms usually translated as "dance," "celebration," or more frequently "doings." The original term *pauau* was used to designate a curing ceremony in an Algonquian language, and did not become popular nationally until the mid-1950s. Although the term was used widely in Oklahoma to designate a week or weekend of singing, dancing, feasting, and other events such as giveaways and trading, it did not receive wide attention until after World War II, during which time many people became highly mobilized, relocated, and came in contact with other people they had never known before. It was no different with American Indians, and I attribute much of what was later known (erroneously, I think) as Pan-Indianism to the high degree of mobility achieved after the war.

Most of the tribes on the Plains, to varying degrees, have been hosting celebrations to which tourists were only incidental. Possibly owing to easier access to the tribes in Oklahoma and the fact that 67 tribes had been removed there since the early nineteenth century, much of what passes as powwow today is derived from Oklahoma, particularly the contests. As I have stated in other works, costumes for the dancers tended to remain tribally oriented for lady dancers (the preferred term on the Southern Plains) but were much more flexible for the male dancers. Later in the book I discuss such costume and dance styles as "fancy" and "straight" dance, "traditional" and "Grass" dance, but the point I want to make here is that for over 40 years I have witnessed not so much a rapid change in Plains Indian musical performance as a consistent return to earlier forms of singing, dancing, and costuming. Just as the late 1980s have witnessed a recurrence of musical, dance, and clothing styles of the 1950s and 1960s, so the same phenomenon has been happening in Indian country.

Continuity and change in American Indian musical performance, whether it is predictable or not (it usually isn't), means that the sum total of tribal cultures that we call American Indian is very much alive and well. Although there certainly are other aspects of culture that contribute to this viability—kinship, religion, economics, and politics—there is no doubt that musical performance is perhaps the most vital because it is the most visible. Much of what one knows about kinship, for example, requires some knowledge of the native language. And many religious ceremonies were or recently have become forbidden to outsiders. Tribal politics is such a specialized form of government that understanding it is almost limited to those actively involved. But music and dance are generally secular; they are open to the general public, frequently not only to watch but also to participate. Even the restrictions placed on non-Indians joining in powwows, which came about largely as a result of the unrest of the 1960s, have been reversed. Last year, one of the best powwows I attended was the second annual International Brotherhood Pow-wow, held in a beautiful setting near the town of Porcupine, South Dakota. People from all over the world attended—people from different tribes, different nations, different ethnic groups—and the sentiment that prevailed for the entire duration of the weeklong celebration was one extremely reminiscent, at least to me, of the later 1940s and 1950s, when drums and dance grounds were open to everyone who had an interest in American Indian culture.

What I hope the essays in the volume will do is provide some background, including the history, the continuity, and the change that I have witnessed in American Indian culture from the perspective of Plains Indian musical performance. Some of the essays, written in the early 1960s, are just as significant today as they were then, but I have revised all of them to indicate precisely what time period I am writing about. I can remember in 1968 I wrote about a new dance craze that had invaded the Lakota reservations from Canada and North Dakota—the Grass dance. It was so different from the traditional dancing I had seen before. There were lithe dancers in fringed and ribboned costumes, porcupine headdresses sporting crests made from plume-tipped choke springs. Moccasins were replaced by sneakers, and many of the dancers wore sunglasses. They bounced and shook as they danced in a "hip" way that I had never seen before. It was soon to be replaced, however, by other styles that my friend and colleague R. D. Theisz was to characterize as the "New Sioux." And that was what replaced the Grass dance, but only for a short time.

In the 1980s, again the younger dancers are out there in heavily fringed costumes, somewhat modified from the 1960s, but they are dancing the same Grass dance with the same trick steps. But there are some significant changes in the songs, and perhaps the 1980s will herald what I consider to be the most significant change in powwow singing ever to be heard, a style that I have witnessed since about 1985 but that seems to be taking hold as we move into the 1990s. Just like the earlier Grass dance, the songs come from the north—Canada, North Dakota, Montana. Like the original Grass dance songs that were sung totally with vocables, these new songs are sung almost entirely with words, and frequently the words are abbreviated so that only someone familiar with the song style can understand them. Moreover, they are sung by nearly all the tribes on the Northern Plains. They are sung mainly by young people, and many of the older generation are opposed to them. Sound familiar? These songs not only contain words, sometimes not even sung in complete sentences (one of the complaints), but they are extremely syncopated and peppy. They are fast, and just as the traditional songs of another era brought the dancers onto the dance floor, these songs, too, make the young people want to dance. Who can say what will replace them (if anything), and who can say, if replaced, when they will return? Perhaps in the year 2010, when in all likelihood powwows will still be the focus of musical performance.

Chapter 1, "The Future Study of American Indian Music," attempts to place Plains music and dance in a broad perspective showing how they have been studied in the past. I am more interested in what is happening on the reservations and Indian communities, a position I call a "reservationist" (as opposed to "preservationist"). The difference between the two positions largely reflects the attitudes of those who see Indian music and dance as thriving cultural forms of expression, and those who would see them as dying out and therefore necessary to salvage.

Chapter 2, "Plains Music," provides a brief history of the study of Plains music, particularly by anthropologists and ethnomusicologists, and also opts for distinguishing between certain geographic and regional styles of music and dance most often identified with the contemporary powwow.

Chapter 3, "War Dance," provides a description of the most popular dance of the powwow along with idiosyncrasies found on the Northern and Southern Plains.

Chapter 4, "Music in Motion," discusses the major differences between what I call "tribalism" and "intertribalism," the latter a term I much prefer over the specious term "pan-Indian" (which I discuss later in the book). I also focus on the diffusion of Plains Indian music and dance, which has been a major subject of study in anthropology since the establishment of the discipline in the United States by Franz Boas.

Chapter 5, "The Powwow," discusses the larger context in which the War dance appears and describes the other types of dances usually found interspersed between War dances.

Chapter 6, "Pan-Indianism Versus Pan-Tetonism," offers the hypothesis that differences in forms of the powwow and regional styles are created not only through repeated performance but also through one's sense of tribal history, religion, material culture, and language, all of which help in part to define music and dance style.

Chapter 7, "Pan-Indianism Reconsidered," is a review of the literature on the concept of Pan-Indianism beginning with James H. Howard's seminal article in 1955 and ending with his 1976 study of the Gourd dance. My point is that a premature concern with the idea of Pan-Indianism really misled and misdirected the study of Plains Indian music and dance by focusing too sharply on what many anthropologists, historians, and ethnomusicologists believed to be a nationalization of American Indians. In the process of following this rather limited position, the fact that individual tribes were still very much concerned with their own sense of ethnic identity was all but obscured, thus creating a need to label any modern developments as "revivalistic" rather than seeing them as a continuum of earlier tribal customs.

Chapter 8, "Songs of the Red Man," Chapter 9, "Toward a Sound Ethnography," and Chapter 10, "'Sioux' Favorites," constitute three discographic review essays that provide descriptions of Plains songs still available on disc and tape from Canyon Records, Indian House, and the now defunct Songs of the Red Man label. In these essays I try to complement the sounds of the singers by adding some notes related to the history and culture of the tribes involved. I have also taken the liberty of providing some translations of songs in Lakota.

Finally, in Chapter 11, "Have Drum, Will Travel," I make some observations on why I think Plains Indian music and dance have received the interest, if not fame, that they have, and why they will continue to symbolize a strong and burgeoning contemporary American Indian culture not only on the Plains but in every corner of the world where American Indians are highly respected, admired, and imitated.

PART I

Plains Indian Music and Dance

Chapter 1

The Future Study of American Indian Music

When one is researching the state of the art of American Indian music and dance, a paradox emerges: just at a time when there appears to be a burgeoning of Plains-style music and dance, both within and outside the Plains culture area, there is a concomitant deficit in the number of researchers currently working in this field. There also is a paucity of research currently being published on American Indian music and dance in general, and on Plains music and dance in particular.

This first paradox gives rise to still another: because there is such a massive inventory of musical collections on hand, mainly as a result of the fieldwork of our intellectual antecedents, if more researchers were sent into the field, it would tend to discourage the badly needed analysis of these data that already have been collected. Finally, whether anthropologists and ethnomusicologists focus on new collections or old, today American Indians themselves, on the Plains and elsewhere, are not only singing and dancing to traditional themes, but they have begun to demonstrate a more academic interest in their own expressive culture in many ways, for the same reasons that earlier antiquarians recorded music—out of a fear that it was about to vanish. So, for American Indian scholars and performers, there is a renewed interest in old songs, that is, those composed and performed for the most part during the earliest reservation period through the first quarter of the twentieth century. This focus on the past has also tended to shift interests expressed by tribal peoples themselves onto music and dance forms which are perceived to be tribal rather than intertribal, sacred instead of secular, traditional rather than modern, and in general, old, not new.

In the following pages what I hope to do is to compare some of our retrospective interests in Plains music with trends of the present in light of casting some reflections of what might be prospects for continuing and future research. I will address some specific problems which may be applicable to studies outside the Plains area, as well as to cultural domains outside the sphere of music and dance.

To this extent, I believe that a Plains perspective is particularly useful and revealing for the following reasons: (a) there has been more published on Plains music and dance than on any other cultural-musical area, if not explicitly, then implicitly;[1] (b) the Plains stereotype in both historical and modern literature and media has had an effect not only on non-Indian publics but also on Indians themselves outside the Plains culture area, and this leads to perhaps the most important consideration; (c) in patterns of music and dance diffusion throughout the United States and Canada, the Plains cultures have contributed much more than they have received, both on reservations and in urban areas.

Perhaps all retrospective and prospective considerations of expressive culture are destined to be argued from two major perspectives: the preservationist on the one hand, the reservationist on the other. By "preservationist," I mean an attitude towards fieldwork and analysis that is largely generated by individual or disciplinary concerns, if not fears, that American Indian music is vanishing, and that all efforts must be made to salvage melodies and rhythms, and choreographic structures, even if it is only to relegate them to archival bins. Implicit in the preservationist approach is a denial of the concept of culture as an ongoing phenomenon capable of transmitting values over generations. The preservationist approach consciously or unconsciously suggests that *real* American Indian culture is pre-reservation, and therefore dead; only modified, impure, bastardized, tainted remnants or vestiges survive.

By "reservationist," I mean an attitude toward music and dance and other cultural domains that is largely concerned with contemporary music, that is, music and attendant cultural domains which not only are contiguous with, but also are often seen to be a product of, the reservation period, a period continuing up through present time, whether Indians live on reservations or not. For the reservationist the concept of culture is taken more literally: American Indian musics are worthy of study despite their historical connections or functional modifications of form and content.

For the preservationist, time is short. For the reservationist, time is not a consideration.

Both attitudes frequently use the same kinds of anthropological and musicological theories and methods: historical, ethnohistorical, evolutionary, structural, and functional. Fortunately, I believe that the preservationist in contemporary times is overshadowed by the reservationist.

From the reservationist perspective, then, one superimposed upon the Plains cultures, I would like to address the following problems discussed over nearly a century of research: (1) the Plains as a culture area versus the Plains as a musical area; (2) the relationship between tribalism and inter-tribalism or, more commonly, Pan-Indianism; (3) Indian music in the cities; (4) the classification of music; (5) the American Indian recording industry; (6) material culture; (7) the relationship between the individual singer and the group in the larger context of the tribe; (8) professionalization of music and dance; and (9) native theories of music and dance as compared with our own.

These categories of problems are not exhaustive, but I do believe that they represent some of the most viable issues in American Indian music and dance which should be considered in future research.

THE PLAINS CULTURE AREA

Depending on one's definition of tribe, and one's historical orientation (i.e., pre- or post-reservation period), there are approximately 30 tribes of American Indians associated with the Great Plains culture area. A more accurate number requires a series of operational definitions, particularly after the establishment of reservations, in order to determine whether or not the term "Sioux," as one example, applies to one or several tribes; or whether one counts the Cheyenne and the Arapaho twice because of their respective northern and southern divisions; or whether the Oto-Missouri are counted as two tribes; and so on. Perhaps even more problems arise if we take

Camp of tipi and wall tents on the Blackfeet Reservation, Montana, ca. 1900–1920. *Courtesy of Smithsonian Office of Anthropology, Bureau of American Ethnology Collection.*

into consideration the culture change over long historic periods at the beginning of which we find other tribes, such as Apache and Wichita, moving into the region from other, equally static culture areas. Another problem deals with the anthropological classification system of American Indian tribes in which often foreign terms are used to label perceptibly stable populations. If these terms were exchanged for tribal self-designations, the classification system would be radically altered.

Despite the problems in nomenclature, all of the tribes have been studied from the perspective of music and dance, but not surprisingly there is less than a desirable qualitative and quantitative corpus of study for all 30. The fact that any study at all exists for all tribes is predicated on the fact that at the turn of the century the Boasians engaged in a number of researches, in this case on the Sun dance and Plains sodalities, which were later published as *Anthropological Papers* of the American Museum of Natural History. In these publications, at least some aspects of music, dance, and material culture, including ceremonial costumes, personal regalia, instruments, and the performance space, are alluded to. In addition, a few of the Plains tribes have been studied both quantitatively and qualitatively. For example, Frances Densmore contributed a great understanding and unmatched corpus of publications which covered (in chronological order of publication) the Teton (1918), the Mandan and Hidatsa (1923), the Pawnee (1929), the Cheyenne and Arapaho (1936), and the Omaha (1944), but these publications are uneven in the coverage of music and dance events, and none equals her other work, most notably on the Chippewa.

Since the publication of these seminal works, Densmore, Fletcher (whose work on the Omaha is the first conscious monograph on Plains music, 1883), and the Boasians have been joined or followed by a multitude of eclectic researchers who have tended to focus on specific problems delimited not only by theoretical (historical) interests but also by topical ones. These eclectic approaches can be characterized as follows:

1. *Tribal,* in which the objective of the research is to describe and analyze what is regarded as the total musical inventory of one particular tribe, such as Densmore has done for the tribes in her works cited above, and more recently by Black Bear and Theisz, whose work on Lakota music and dance may be considered somewhat of a landmark in that the entire book is bilingual (Black Bear and Theisz 1976).

2. *Generic,* in which the research focuses on genres of song or dance found among a number of different tribes, such as those published by Colby (1895) and Mooney (1896) on songs of the Ghost dance, and by Fenner (1976) and Howard (1976) on the Gourd dance.

3. *Tribal-generic,* the most ubiquitous category, in which the research focuses on one genre of one tribe, such as Dorsey's work on the Arapaho Sun dance (1903) and the Ponca Sun dance (1905).

4. *Regional,* perhaps best exemplified by James H. Howard's work on Pan-Indianism in Oklahoma (1955) and his subsequent work on Northern Plains Grass dance costumes (1960), and my work on the relationship between Pan-Indianism and Pan-Tetonism (1968).

Standing Elk, Ponca. *Photo by DeLancy Gill, February 1914, Ponca Reservation, Nebraska. Courtesy of Smithsonian Office of Anthropology, Bureau of American Ethnology Collection.*

5. *Regional-generic,* perhaps best characterized by Norman Feder's research on the origin of the Oklahoma Forty-nine (1964).

6. *Culture-area,* in which research objectives are addressed to the entire culture area, represented mainly by classificatory problems such as those dealt with by Herzog (1928), Roberts (1936), Nettl (1954), and Powers (1980a).

There is a major agreement among anthropologists that the Plains deserves to be classified as a bona fide culture area, although there is perhaps less agreement on how the Plains should be subdivided into regions. However, ethnomusicologists tend to combine the Plains and Southwest culture areas into one musical area largely on the basis of the similarities in song structure rather than on other cultural similarities. In Chapter 2, I argue for a reclassification which disengages the Plains from the Southwest and, based on similarities of configurations of songs, dances, and attendant material culture, suggest a subdivision of the Plains musical area based on more contemporary styles of music and dance.

In this classification system, the northern and southern distinctions are based on *geocultural* considerations. Within each geocultural area are stylistically distinctive *regional* categories. Within each region are *traditions,* each corresponding to the individual tribes within each region.

In the future, I believe it would be useful to examine more closely the relationship between songs, dances, and attendant costumes and musical instruments as the basis for classification, rather than any one of these variables independent of the others. Further attempts to classify music and dance in the Plains area must reconcile the differences between anthropologists and ethnomusicologists, and very definitely consider alternative classification systems suggested by American Indian scholars themselves.

To this end it may be worthwhile to consider the reservation on the Northern Plains, the Indian community in Oklahoma, or urban centers in the case of both, as units of analytical focus, a practice which precludes the older one of considering the tribe as the essential unit. In such an approach, it is anticipated that reservations with similar tribal backgrounds will show more similar traits than those exhibited in the larger regional or geocultural areas, for instance, Pan-Tetonism as opposed to Northern Plains regionalism, which I discuss in Chapter 6.

TRIBALISM VS. INTERTRIBALISM

Since the study of Plains music has been organized on the basis of theoretical interests, or schools of thought, it is not surprising that the majority of works, reflecting the Boasian persuasion, are historical and descriptive with an emphasis on distance anthropology. The unit of analysis here is the tribe, and this point of view continues from the earliest studies at the turn of the century until 1955, the date of Howard's seminal work on Pan-Indianism.[2] This date also corresponds to a time in which there began an interaction between Northern and Southern Plains tribes, because at approximately this time there was a strong influence of the Oklahoma powwow complex on Northern Plains reservations. This complex soon began to become competitive with the so-called North Dakota influence, actually North Dakota Lakota, Dakota, Cree, and Plains Ojibwa, as well as their Canadian counterparts, whose influences clashed with the Oklahoma complex on the middle Plains areas, mainly in South Dakota.

Howard's article on Oklahoma Pan-Indianism clearly marks a shift in theoretical interest from historical particularism to cultural neo-evolutionism, mainly the product of Whitean theory applied to American Indian expressive culture, a theory partly inspired by a rash of interest in acculturation studies spearheaded by Robert Redfield, Ralph Linton, and Melville Herskovits in the 1930s.[3] It is perhaps appropriate to regard this shift in theoretical interests as from one focusing on tribalism to one concerned chiefly with intertribalism, a perceived state of human evolution in which once tribally distinct traits begin to amalgamate, mainly as a result of the proximity of Indian reservations and communities, particularly in the Southern Plains.

The traits most frequently identified are those associated with music, dance, and dance costumes, and their particular configuration as they appear in the powwow. To a lesser extent the process of amalgamating cultural traits is extended to the political and economic arena, in many ways more successfully. "Powwow," as the term is used in the Southern Plains, designates a period of time—from roughly one day to one week—in which individuals, from one tribe or many, gather to participate in traditional singing, dancing, giveaways, and feasts. The most popular dances are the War dance, Round dance, Gourd dance, Two-step, Stomp dance, and Forty-nine, along with a number of stylized specialty dances such as Snake and Buffalo dance, and occasionally, when visitors are present, Shield dance and Hoop dance. The same dances, to which characteristic tribal dances are added, appear at such events as the American Indian Exposition (locally "Indian Fair") at Anadarko, Oklahoma. There are two major stylistic contrasts on the Southern Plains, the fancy dance and the straight dance, the former roughly associated with western Oklahoma and the latter with northern Oklahoma.

Part of the powwow is devoted to competitions for both sexes and all ages, sometimes graded, and winners receive substantial amounts of prize money as well as prestige.

The term "powwow" did not reach the Northern Plains until 1955, along with much of the Southern Plains complex. However, the Grass dance format which served as the prototype for the Oklahoma powwow already existed on the Northern Plains along with some of the same dances, such as War dance, Round dance, and local variations of Two-step (Rabbit dance and Owl dance), although it might be stated that all powwows in both regions tend to take on tribal or subregional variations. Formats for the powwow have been discussed by Howard (1985) and by me (1968), and an excellent synthesis of costuming has been written by Koch (1977).

The point I would like to make here is that so-called Pan-Indian studies become essentially the only approach to the study of American Indian music that complements or extends any real anthropological theory. This theory is multilinear evolution, and to this end Howard, as its foremost exponent in Plains studies, sees Pan-Indianism as a stage of cultural evolution immediately preceding total assimilation of the American Indian, a subject to which several chapters of this book, particularly Chapter 7, are devoted.

I have argued elsewhere that there is no empirical evidence that Pan-Indianism is in fact a stage, nor has there been any overwhelming evidence since 1955 that it takes any particular direction toward unification of tribally discrete traits. I find it more useful to regard tribalism and intertribalism as two coexisting analytical paradigms in which tribalism, a tendency toward maintaining tribal distinction, becomes indicative of tradition, cultural identity, and continuity in culture, while intertribalism, the tendency toward exchanging cultural traits between tribes and between the Euroamerican society, becomes indicative of modernity, social identity, and cultural change. Stated another way, tribalism underscores the relationships between individuals of the same society within the context of what is perceived to be a bounded domain, the tribe; intertribalism under-scores the relationships between individuals across tribal bound-aries. Tribalism is a statement about cultural identity; intertribalism is one about social identity. They stand in a dialectical relationship to one another.

Additionally, I find that we often conflate the terms "Pan-Indian-ism," "diffusion," "acculturation," and the extreme form of the latter, "assimilation." At best, when sorted out, these terms are descriptive of processes and are not in themselves theories. None of these ideas are as powerful as evolutionary or neo-evolutionary theory to explain continuity and change in American Indian music and dance, and other cultural domains, in any analytical way. I see these terms historically as standing in some dialectical relationship, operating as compromises between historical particularism on the one hand and evolutionary theory on the other. If, in fact, these terms are analogous, then there is no reason to assume that, say, the Grass dance, or powwow complex, is particularly unique. Rather, we may investigate such institutions as the Sun dance and Ghost dance as products of tribal contacts over the entire Plains historical continuum. The interchange of tribal traits on the Plains or else-where is not so much the result of a breakdown in tribal distinctive-ness as it is perhaps the *cause* of the Plains Indian culture, a culture initially made up of the shreds and patches of earlier cultures living in different environments and lasting only some 200 years.

Thus acculturation or any other analogy *is* the process of human evolution, one analogous to the process of differential gene distribu-tion in biological evolution.[4] To this end, there is a need to evaluate the Pan-Indian literature which has preoccupied anthropology and ethnomusicology since the mid 1950s. Despite my criticisms, it is perhaps the most useful application of a general theory to Plains music and dance because it deals with the dynamics of cultural evolution.

THE URBAN CONTINUUM

Here I would like to consider the relationship between what might be regarded as the center and the periphery of the Plains culture area, keeping in mind the tribal-intertribal distinctions to which I have just alluded.

Assiniboine dancers from the Fort Belnap Reservation dressed for a Grass dance, 1906. *Photo by Sumner W. Matteson. Courtesy of Smithsonian Office of Anthropology, Bureau of American Ethnology Collection.*

By "center," I mean the total number of reservations and off-reservation communities on the Plains that participate in traditional music, both composition and performance. By "periphery," I mean the total number of urban areas into which traditional music and dance from the Plains are transmitted. Important here is that some of these urban areas are on the Plains proper and exhibit strong tribal or intertribal characteristics. Others, however, are located outside the Plains area, and today it is safe to say that nearly every urban area exhibits some characteristic of Plains music and dance, including the farthest reaches of the United States, from New York City to Los Angeles and San Francisco, from Chicago to New Orleans. The farther one travels from the center, the more diffuse the Plains musical characteristics become, often resulting in total structural and functional distortions of what was once indisputably Plains.

At one time it was rather simple to observe and identify the reservation and off-reservation communities that had the strongest influences on urban centers such as Tulsa and Oklahoma City on the Southern Plains, and Denver and Bismarck on the Northern Plains. But the migration of Indians to the cities is making this simple picture extremely complex, and lest we fall into the trap of continuing to distance anthropology and ethnomusicology, we are likely to miss an important development in the continuing diffusion of Plains music.

We can begin by regarding the relationships between core and periphery as a reticular map in the process identifying the loci of tribal and intertribal events, populations, and musical and dance influences. I believe that we will begin to see just how complex the variations of even tribalism are from one city to the next. These complexities are frequently attributed to tribal or regional styles which are often regarded as incompatible despite the fact that diverse tribal singers and dancers congregate in the same locus. In Denver, for example, there is currently a biweekly powwow joined in by Northern and Southern Plains peoples. It has been necessary to alternate sponsorship so that at each powwow, a Northern or a Southern Plains drum controls the event. The differences between the two styles are largely predicated on the tempo of the drum (very fast for Southern Plains and slower for Northern), the number of renditions of songs (fewer for the Southern Plains), and the relative pitch of songs (higher for the Northern Plains), the configurations of which enunciate esthetic as well as stylistic preferences of the respective regional participants.

On the other hand, Southern Plains cities still reflect Southern Plains esthetics, and the same is true in the Northern Plains, except for an increasing desire to distinguish between traditional and intertribal (the same distinction as my tribal-intertribal). Often the powwow formats are conceptually divided between old and modern music and dance.

The lines that connect these urban junctions of the reticular map are perhaps old trails traveled by the same people over and over, back and forth, over centuries. But who are the people? What musical and dance ideas do they carry with them to the cities? To what extent do only a few itinerant musicians have immense influence on the musics of many urban areas (I am thinking here of the influences of Ponca singers from the Southern Plains, and Badlands singers from the Northern Plains who have good reputations). Finally, what musical ideas, if any, are brought back to the center from the urban areas? That is, in the dialectical relationship between tribalism and intertribalism, what features from the intertribal sphere are fed back into the tribal sphere?

I believe that the newest frontier of Plains music studies will be found in these relationships between center and periphery. Studies of other types of music, say, jazz, have produced typologies such as West Coast, Kansas City, New Orleans, and Chicago jazz. Perhaps these subregional or urban variations of Plains music and dance may be viewed from the same kind of perspective, and result in similar typologies.

THEORY AND ETHNOTHEORY

A final prospectus for the study of Plains music, and implicitly all native musics of the world including our own, is what I discussed in the paper "Oglala Song Terminology,"[5] which addresses itself to the question of how people structure their perception of reality and the manner in which they verbalize about it. Of course here the subject matter is music, and particularly ethnotheories of music and related domains.

Anyone who has embarked on the field adventure knows that

given enough time and enough tape, American Indian singers are quite capable of expounding verbally about the significance of the songs they have recorded, or are about to record. Most of this exegesis is related to what Boas regarded as the native's proclivity to perpetuate culture, not analyze it, and thus most frequently we are likely to hear a native theoretician articulate the historical significance of the song or songs under consideration, who composed them, under what circumstances, how the songs are evaluated by singers and/or dancers, how old they are, how popular they are, whether they were bought, sold, or otherwise exchanged, foreign influence, and so on ad infinitum.

But along with this historical exegesis, it is unlikely that the natives have no more to say about a cultural domain that plays such a significant part in their everyday lives. It is also unlikely that we will begin to understand this significance unless we begin to investigate these verbalized domains, using theories and methods from other disciplines.

The larger theoretical underpinnings and their implied significance and insignificance have been stated clearly by Feld (1974) and Nattiez (1975), both of whom are interested in structural, symbolic, or semiotic approaches to the study of music, and both of whom are critical of using these methods uncritically. It seems that interdisciplinary, or nonanthropological and nonethnomusicological, theories and methods should be a welcome addition to our own interests, ideas that tend to complement and inspire rather than challenge or refute, although either way these new methods will be refreshing.

Our question is to what extent these other disciplines can help pose new questions about the scientific and humanistic study of world musics. We should expect that, for example, linguistic models of music can be helpful, but not because of a necessarily inherent relationship between language and music, although this may prove to be the case from a bioevolutionary perspective. We should, rather, learn to be discreet enough to employ those linguistic models which do in fact help explain musical problems, and at the same time have the courage to discard those models which are irrelevant.

Similarly, structural-functional models may prove to be valuable as long as we use them not because of their faddishness but because they tell us something more about patterns of thoughts and relationships between cultural domains, and do so more powerfully than other models.

There is still an amazing deficit of ethnomusicological theory that addresses itself to problems raised by biology, sociobiology, neuroanatomy, physiology, and biocultural evolution. I recognize that some ethnomusicologists and musicologists are becoming interested in these fields, but we are only beginning to make a mark in these interdisciplinary endeavors.

I think these new ideas can be particularly useful to the study of American Indian music and to my own interest, Plains music. Nowhere else do we find the kind of explosive music with its attendant impact on other cultural areas as we do in the Plains. My favorite analog is the geological notion of quaquaversality, in which dynamic change occurs in the center of the geologic formation, hurling shock waves in every possible direction unevenly and with varying degrees of intensity. Such is the explosive nature of Plains music.

New ideas may help address or readdress some of the most interesting and still unanswered questions in music: How do people classify their musical universe? What is the nature of musical composition? If music is expressive of culture in general, then what structural and functional aspects of culture does it express? To what extent can we speak of a technical language of native music, one employed by singers and composers themselves? Is music considered a cultural domain in all societies, or might it be a natural one?[6] Is there anything more than a contextual difference between sacred and secular music? All these are examples of questions asked, and sometimes successfully answered, with respect to domains outside the musical and dance sphere.

Perhaps analysts of American Indian music and other musics of the world require still another epicyclic turn to move back on ourselves, back to Boasian edicts of the turn of the century to get inside the natives' head, not only to marvel at the melodies and rhythms that American Indian peoples produce, in a never-ending stream of self- and cultural expression, but also to marvel at the complexity of American Indian thought processes that give rise to that panhuman expression of humanity, the natural or cultural things of life we call music and dance.

Chapter 2

Plains Music

In the early studies of comparative musicology, Erich von Hornbostel regarded the vocal music of the Plains Indians as possessing a characteristic presumed to be "racially inherent among all Indians" (quoted in Nettl 1954:24). Von Hornbostel's assessment of music is analogous to the ubiquitous position assigned to Iroquoian kinship terminology by Lewis Henry Morgan. Today, anthropologists would not consider either proposition valid, but it might be refreshing to reconsider von Hornbostel's premature conclusions as a form of prophecy rather than of scientific theory. Plains Indian music, and certain forms of dance, while not "racially inherent," have in fact become socially heritable signs of American Indian cultural vitality and identity, not only on the Plains but in other Indian communities as well.

Indeed, since the turn of the century, Plains music and dance have become symbolic of American Indian resistance to wholesale adoption of Euroamerican culture, and it is partly through these particular cultural forms that American Indian values manifest themselves. Because of the influential nature of Plains music and dance, and its association with social, political, and economic interests of many other U.S. tribes, a clearer understanding of these culturally expressive domains will enable us to better understand contemporary American Indian societies. Since music and dance occupy a preeminent position, and are at once a manifestation of technology and ideology, one would suspect that they have a potential for leading to understanding of the integration of American Indian society in very specific ways. However, as I will underscore throughout this book, their integrative function has not been consciously studied. This perhaps is owing to the nature of American anthropology in the early days rather than to any oversight on the part of the investigators. There is still time to rectify this seeming neglect of tangible and measurable data.

The anthropological study of Plains music and dance began with the establishment of the American Museum of Natural History, the Peabody Museum, and the Bureau of American Ethnology. Perhaps the first conscious effort at a description of tribal music is Alice C. Fletcher's "A Study of Omaha Indian Music" (1893). Studies of this sort, through the 1940s, were dominated by Alice Fletcher and her collaborator, Francis LaFlesche, Natalie Curtis (1907), George Herzog (1928), Helen H. Roberts (1936), and the outstanding comparative musicologist Frances Densmore (1916–1944), the quantity of whose work has never been equalled.

The ethnomusicological research of this period was supplemented by a score of Boasians who collected data on the Plains Sun dance and Plains sodalities, which were published in the *Anthropological Papers* of the American Museum of Natural History. Their focus was on the description of tribal traits, while secondary emphasis was laid upon the current theoretical interest in diffusion. Historical and comparative summaries were published by Lowie (1916) and Spier (1921a).

This work led beyond scientific discourse to the popularization of American Indian expressive culture. Ethnomusicologists inspired such composers as Charles Skilton, Horace Miller, Thurlow Lieurance, and Edward McDowell to compose and orchestrate popular and symphonic music based on native American themes. This particular "backwash" of Native American culture has been treated aptly by Hallowell (1957). The interpretation of Indian dancing, much of which was based on early anthropological studies, became almost the exclusive domain of Indian lorists, camp directors, and youth organizations through the writings of Ernest T. Seton (1927), Daniel Beard (1909), Ralph Hubbard (1927), Julian Saloman (1928), Julia Buttree (1930), and Bernard S. Mason (1944). It is not my purpose to dwell on the history of the study of Plains music and dance (see particularly Densmore 1941 and Nettl 1954), but I men-

Arikara Grass dancers, Fort Berthold Agency, December 6, 1886. *Photo collected by Major A. J. Gifford, agent at Fort Berthold, Dakota Territory. Courtesy of Smithsonian Office of Anthropology, Bureau of American Ethnology Collection.*

tion these early investigators in a particular context. Historically, approaches to music and dance have been somewhat divided between anthropology and ethnomusicology, and each respective discipline has generated a further dichotomy between scientific and popular interpretation. The distinction between scientific and popular has often been misread as professional versus amateur, but the latter category often compensates for professional deficiencies. Comprehensive study of American Indian music and dance, historically and culturally, thus requires an examination of both bodies of literature (cf. Feder 1954–1960; Powers 1964–1966, 1988; Morgan 1966–1968; Heriard 1967–; and Stewart 1967–1974).

Despite formidable collections of musical data—Frances Densmore alone contributed 3,591 cylinders to the Library of Congress—there are still large gaps in our knowledge of Plains music and dance. In the 1950s, there was a steady decline in the number of

Omaha dancer. *Photo by F. N. Bentley, Pender, Nebraska. Taken prior to 1907. Courtesy of Smithsonian Office of Anthropology, Bureau of American Ethnology Collection.*

published articles including pure description of expressive culture. Aside from Densmore's earlier monographs, there are no musical ethnographies for the Plains equivalent to Merriam's (1967) work on the Flathead except for Nettl's four-part series on Blackfeet musical culture (1967a, 1967b, 1968a, 1968b). Conversely, no synthetic works even of a descriptive nature have been produced (although McAllester's [1949] work on Peyote music includes Plains examples). Perhaps the lack of theoretical and methodological interest is partially explained by technological achievements in recording apparatus. The 1950s saw a proliferation of commercial recording companies aimed at supplying the American Indian market. Folkways, Indian House, American Indian Soundchief, and Canyon Records, in particular, each of which maintains a large inventory of Plains music, can perhaps be regarded as the new ethnographers of music. The recordings provide a useful historical index, but most lack any synthesis for comparative analysis. They constitute, in fact, another form of raw data which is accumulating in overwhelming proportions. A few recordings are reviewed and analyzed in such journals as *Ethnomusicology,* but time and space limitations make it impossible to keep up with their production.

The anthropological study of music and dance on the Plains, or elsewhere in Indian America, is paradoxical. Unlike most other social and cultural categories, music and dance are neatly bounded, highly visible and audible, and readily performed. In most cases, even a moderately trained anthropologist can learn when a song or dance begins, reaches a climax, and ends. One can learn a great deal by simple observation, and some researchers have become proficient in music and dance skills.[1] There is nothing secretive about music and dance, although associated values may be private and difficult to understand. In short, an anthropologist can easily come to know or even perform music and dance. But—here is the paradox—the more anthropologists know about music and dance, the less they seem to accomplish with accumulated data. Due to its unending emphasis on collection because of the fear that Indian cultures were dying, anthropology has reached the stage where it labors under sheer volume with little hope of achieving even such preliminary steps toward analysis as identification, classification, and distribution studies. There is little or no work on the process of composition, native terminology, the evaluation of music and dance, esthetics, performance standards, tribal classifications, native theories of instrument manufacture, musicianship, and, particularly, the relationship with other sociocultural domains: kinship, economics, politics, and religion. Of course music and dance have been described and put into some kind of context, but analysis rarely does more than call our attention to the fact that they are unquestionably "functional."

Little has been done in understanding the structural relationships between expressive domains. And if music and dance are indeed critical indices of expressive culture, we remain hard pressed to discover just what aspects of society and culture they express. Hence, throughout the book, I will offer a summary of the anthropological status of Plains music and dance, and suggest some theoretical and methodological considerations for future study. This is done in the belief that knowledge about music and dance may help us comprehend other aspects of American Indian cultures, both historical and contemporary. I will focus on problems of understanding contemporary music and dance, particularly the somewhat overworked notion of Pan-Indianism.

TYPOLOGICAL CONSIDERATIONS

For an understanding of the relationships between music and dance, as well as between these categories and other sociocultural domains, the Plains culture area is best divided into northern and southern areas. This, of course, is consistent with anthropological practice but not with that of ethnomusicology. The latter discipline essentially studies such structural features of music as melody, scale, range, and tempo (Nettl 1954, 1956), musical composition, and performance. Using the criterion of "vocal tenseness," for example, ethnomusicologists have combined the Plains and Southwest culture areas into the Plains-Pueblo musical area (Herzog 1928; Roberts 1936; Nettl 1954). Here we must consider the age-old problem of "traits." Both classifications result largely from the arbitrary selection of isolated traits rather than the relationship between cultural categories. Both are useful, of course, depending on the researcher's specific interests, but I prefer to break with ethnomusicological tradition, and opt for the Northern/Southern Plains distinction as the most useful for the understanding of music in a wider cultural context.

Between these two geocultural areas we should imagine a boundary line running roughly through the middle of Nebraska. Northern and Southern music and dance styles are quite disparate, but they do tend to overlap and diffuse. Diffusion occurs mainly from north to south in music style, and from south to north in dance style, a phenomenon to which I shall return. The most intensive area of diffusion, in which we find that the most rapid change in both styles occurs, is logically the reservation center of the Plains, mainly Pine Ridge and Rosebud, South Dakota. Because of their geographic centrality, much new music and dance filters through both reservations, undergoing some modification through this Siouan catalyst. Additionally, urban areas such as Bismarck, Chicago, Denver, Minneapolis, and Oklahoma City are centers of rapid diffusion.

The Northern and Southern Plains may be divided into regional areas which largely correspond to linguistic families and tribal affiliations (Powers 1969, 1971). Most of these have evolved out of the removal of American Indians from earlier homelands to their present reservations and communities. Non-Plains peoples live on both the Northern and Southern Plains, and are influencing and being influenced by indigenous Plains tribes. This is particularly important in understanding the current exchange of music and dance forms. At the national level most intertribal music and dance—wherever performed—is essentially Plains in style. Throughout this book, I will concentrate on music and dance of the Plains proper, rather than influences upon it from outside the Plains area, recognizing that the relationship of esoteric and exoteric forms of the same music and dance structures is worthy of future research.

In speaking of Plains music, then, I am referring to music and dance that are indigenous to the area from the establishment of the reservations up through the present. Tribal distributions are quite different in each geocultural area. In the north we find relatively large homogenous tribes or confederations, such as the Blackfeet, Crow, and Lakota. The reservations are relatively isolated compared with the Indian communities of the Southern Plains, where we find smaller Plains and Prairie tribes commingled with tribes removed from other culture areas. Most of the latter were settled in Oklahoma, and Southern Plains style is perhaps better known as "Oklahoma style."

The geographic distribution of Southern Plains communities, mainly in Oklahoma, facilitated the rapid exchange of dance, music, and material culture related to both forms. But on the Northern Plains the exchange between regions and tribes has been much slower. The essential Southern Plains style, performed at intertribal functions, is divided into Fancy Dancing and Straight Dancing. These styles are regional in nature: Fancy Dancing is primarily associated with western Oklahoma and Straight Dancing with northern Oklahoma.[2] On the Northern Plains are four regional styles: (1) North Dakota, (2) Blackfeet, (3) Crow, and (4) South Dakota (see Table 1).[3]

The distinctions between geocultural and regional forms of music and dance are stylistic. Within regional styles we may also speak of traditional tribal styles. Style is differentiated not on the basis of song or dance structure but on that of interrelationships between music, dance, and, importantly, related material culture (specifically musical instruments and dance costumes). In the past, ethnomusicologists determined style solely on the basis of structural features of the song. The Plains style has been further characterized on the basis of songs being strophic, that is, containing sections or phrases which tend to become longer toward the end of the strophe. Other diagnostic features include average range of a tenth, frequency of tetratonic scales, scale intervals of major seconds and minor thirds, melodic movement of the terrace type, and rhythm dominated by four or five durational values. The majority of songs are accompanied by rhythmic instruments with only a simple pulse (Nettl 1954:28–29). Songs have been described as being of the incomplete repetition type, but essentially this is a feature of performance rather than song structure (cf. Chapter 6).

Ethnomusicologists find three major categories of musical instruments in both Plains areas: membranophones, aerophones, and idiophones. There are no vibraphones such as the Apache fiddle. Musical instruments are critical to discerning regional and tribal styles, but they have not been regarded as such. The same holds for dance costumes. Any style, then, should be defined as the pattern of

Table 1 Typology of Plains Music and Dance Styles

A. Northern
  1. Blackfeet
     a. Blackfeet proper
     b. Piegan
     c. Blood
     d. Sarcee
  2. North Dakota
     a. Assiniboine
     b. Gros Ventre (Atsina)
     c. Mandan
     d. Plains Cree
     e. Plains Ojibwa
     f. Canadian, Montana, North Dakota Sioux
  3. Crow
  4. South Dakota
     a. Northern Arapahoe
     b. Northern Cheyenne
     c. South Dakota Sioux
B. Southern Plains
  1. Western Oklahoma (primarily Fancy dancing)
     a. Apache (Chiricahua)
     b. Caddo
     c. Comanche
     d. Kiowa
     e. Kiowa-Apache
     f. Southern Arapaho
     g. Southern Cheyenne
     h. Wichita
  2. Northern Oklahoma (primarily Straight dancing)
     a. Iowa
     b. Kansa
     c. Omaha
     d. Osage
     e. Oto-Missouri
     f. Pawnee
     g. Ponca
     h. Quapaw
     i. Tonkawa

interrelationships between structural song features, dance (or other functional equivalent), instrument(s), and costuming for male and female singers and dancers. Such considerations immediately divorce the Pueblo style from that of the Plains while reaffirming the cultural similarities between tribes on the Plains which led to the original formulation of the Plains culture area. This reconsideration of style allows comparison among tribal and intertribal variations of music and dance, as well as other related social and cultural categories. Table 1 (above) summarizes these considerations.

We may regard the distinction between Northern and Southern Plains as geocultural; the distinction between Blackfeet, North Dakota, Crow, South Dakota, and western and northern Oklahoma as regional; and the tribal distinctions within each regional style as traditional. In one case (the Crow) the regional and traditional style are coterminous. These typologies of course mean nothing in themselves, but may lead to more fruitful studies of the relation between expressive culture and those aspects of society they express. The structural features of music, dance, and material culture may be seen as analogs of other structural features of society, such as kinship, marriage, and levels of group organization.

The typological approach to music and dance, of course, has the disadvantages inherent in any typology. It does not deal with the dynamics and interchange of music and dance between geocultural, regional, and traditional groups. Understanding this interchangeability is, of course, essential to understanding the notion of the burdensome concept of Pan-Indianism.

In summary, I regard the Plains area as a monadic unit and subdivide it into environments in the following way (see Table 1):

1. Northern and Southern Plains are regarded as geocultural divisions, and I suggest that there is a homogeneity within each division which cannot be found at any higher level of contrast.

2. Each of the two geocultural divisions is subdivided into regions, each region being represented by a cluster of tribes. The Northern geocultural area is divided into four regions: Blackfeet, North Dakota, Crow, and South Dakota; and the Southern area is divided into two regions: western and northern Oklahoma. These divisions suggest that there is a homogeneity found within each

region which cannot be found at any higher or lower level of contrast.

3. Each of the respective regional areas is subdivided into traditions. These subdivisions represent the minimal unit of classification and are synonymous with tribe.

Style, the typological diagnostic feature, is defined as the total configuration of structural features of music, dance, musical instruments, and dance costumes, and their relationships to each other—and the ideologies and values underlying each of the structural features. One must also include the structural and functional features of the performance of music and dance and related categories.

Now, I would like to turn to the single most popular aspect of Plains music and dance, the War dance.

Chapter 3

War Dance

War dance today is the most vital and popular of all Plains Indian music and dance. Its importance may be measured by its widespread diffusion on the Northern and Southern Plains, its penetration into other music areas, its influence on intertribal celebrations, and its accelerated proliferation since the turn of the century. War dance is the nucleus of today's tribal and intertribal powwows both on reservations and in urban Indian communities.

Much of today's War dance is an amalgamation of many tribal styles of the Northern and Southern Plains. Within these two major geocultural subdivisions remains an older form of music and dance style which is a remnant of the Grass dance and related ceremonies which were popular on the Northern and Southern Plains in the 1870s. This older form has characteristic music and dance which may be termed the "classic" style. Therefore, while the "northern style" is popular on the Northern Plains, there remain northern tribes who still sing and dance in the classic style. The same is true on the Southern Plains.[1]

NOMENCLATURE

The term "War dance" is somewhat specious. It generally does not relate to warfare with the exception of some dances performed in honor of war heroes. These are usually restricted to the reservation areas and are comprised of word songs. At intertribal celebrations, the term "War dance" suffices, but on reservations and in other Indian communities, we find that War dance is known by other names. Among the Lakota on the Pine Ridge and Rosebud reservations, it is called "Omaha dance," because the dance was historically learned from the Omaha tribe; among the Shoshoni and Arapaho it is known as the "Wolf dance," the wolf being associated with the warrior or scout; the Lakota of Standing Rock as well as the Blackfeet, Cree, Assiniboine, and Three Affiliated Tribes call it "Grass dance," a term used by many of the Northern Plains tribes.

On the Southern Plains, while the dance is known generically as war dancing, there is a distinction made between the fast, or "Fancy," dance of the Kiowa, Comanche, Kiowa-Apache, Cheyenne, and Arapaho, and the more conservative, or classic "Straight" dance of the northern Oklahoma tribes. Many of the ceremonies connected with the Osage, Pawnee, and other styles of dancing can be traced directly to the Grass dance of the Northern Plains.

The popularity of the term probably originated with the advent of wild west shows when non-Indian impresarios were coining promotional slogans to attract the imaginations of the general public. However it originated, the term remained and is currently used or understood by Indians themselves.

In order to understand the diffusion of War dance, some discussion of its morphology and style is necessary. The diffusion process, as we shall learn, dictates that sometimes the song and dance style must be modified as it moves from reservation to reservation. In learning about the morphology of the War dance song, we will understand what sections of the songs are modified and how. But first, let us attempt to broadly define War dance and music and describe its prominent features.

"War dance" is a generic term applied by Plains Indians themselves to a form of group dance in which individuals perform freestyle movements. The dance has little or no formal routine or pattern; rather, the dancers move spontaneously in various directions within the dance area. There is a tendency for the entire body of dancers to move en masse around the center of the dance area in a clockwise or counterclockwise direction. In the Northern Plains the direction is usually counterclockwise, while the opposite is true on the Southern Plains. Some special songs dictate a contrary ruling to the normal direction of dance.

While the dance is primarily for men, women participate to a

People performing the Rabbit dance in the home of Chief James Red Cloud, Pine Ridge, South Dakota. Photo was taken ca. 1930. The woman on the right with a floral shawl is Mrs. Charles (Laura) Red Cloud. *Courtesy of the U.S. Indian Service.*

lesser degree, either dancing in place or moving clockwise or counterclockwise, using conservative steps. The degree to which the women perform varies from tribe to tribe, as does the direction of their movement. On the Pine Ridge and Rosebud reservations, the women dance on the outside of the men in a clockwise (opposite) direction, while in Oklahoma they normally dance in the same direction as the men, usually mingled with the male dancers.[2]

The War dance is performed in traditional or modified traditional dance costumes. Generally the costumes are similar, although definite tribal styles still exist. The costumes generally complement the characteristic movements of dancers: abrupt changes of posture, angular torso and arm movements, rapid and erratic nodding of the head, and a variety of steps which coincide with the tempo of the song and drum. Many dancers carry eagle-bone or metal whistles which they blow during certain parts of the song.[3]

On reservations War dances are performed year round but reach a crescendo between May and September, when they are danced outdoors in large brush arbors. In the winter they are danced in community halls. War dances are also performed in conjunction with religious observations or patriotic holidays, but are not necessarily religious or patriotic themselves. War dancing may also be found as focal points of Indian traveling shows or tourist attractions, and is also performed regularly—usually monthly—in cities where there are large Indian populations.

The melody is characterized by descending, pentatonic scales. The pitch of the song is generally higher in the north than in the south. There is a variety of voice characteristics: in the north songs are sung falsetto at the beginning, dropping into raspy, throaty registers. In the south there is an absence of falsetto but an abundance of nasal, quavering tones. In the classic styles of the north one hears stressed vocables resembling falsetto shouts or yelps.

Depending on the text, three kinds of War dance songs exist: (1) those sung with vocables or burden syllables only; (2) those sung with words only; and (3) those sung with both vocables and words.[4]

The songs are sung in unison by a group of male singers standing or seated around a bass dance drum, each using a drumstick. They are assisted by a few women who sing an octave above them, their voices trailing behind the men's after each chorus. The average group consists of six to eight men, sometimes more.

On the Southern Plains, one "drum" (group of singers) provides the music for a War dance, but on the Northern Plains I have seen as many as 23 drums at one gathering. When there is more than one, the song groups alternate.

The tempo varies depending on the song. For this reason they are sometimes referred to as slow, medium, or fast War dances. The rhythm is pulsating, and increases and decreases in volume intermittently. Accented duple beats and secondary accented beats occur both at specific junctures and spontaneously.

There is a definite synchronization of voice and drum, though to the Western-oriented ear they appear to be independent. While, in some instances, the drumbeat coincides precisely with the utterance of a vocable, it more often occurs "between" the vocables. The drumbeat slightly precedes the voice; if we examine the beginnings and endings of War dance songs, we find that the drum is struck an instant before the voice begins and ends an instant before the voice. When the song accelerates or decelerates, there is a constant relationship between the voice and the drum.

The most significant trait of all War dance songs is the similarity of the song form. Whether the War dance song is sung on the Northern or Southern Plains, or even beyond the periphery of the Plains area, the internal structures of the songs are identical. While word songs are still composed, most War dance songs are comprised entirely of vocables. Like the form, the vocable is similar in all regions, but because the vocable structure of a song is governed by language, the vocables change (cf. Chapter 5).

Generally, in the diffusion process, sounds which are foreign to a tribe are substituted. The relationship between language and music, or vocable and music, and vocable and language is important to note, as it plays a major role in the diffusion process.

COMPOSITION AND ADAPTATION

Diffusion begins with the composition or adaptation of a song. War dance songs are composed by individuals who are established in the Indian community as singers or "song-makers." In the case of new songs, the composer creates the melody, vocables, and words in

accordance with a desired tempo. His inspiration is derived either
from supernatural sources, such as dreams, or vision quests, or
through conscious creativity. In either case, he is in essence compos-
ing against a list of predetermined standards: scale, vocables, language, and form. Singers have told me that they receive inspiration
from such phenomena as the hum of tires on a road, the whisper of
wind in the trees, or the conscious creation of a rhythmic pattern
such as beating two rocks or sticks together. In all cases the inspiration seems to originate in the deliberation on monotonous, sound-
producing phenomena.

In cases of song adaptation, the composer may add words to a
song which already exists with vocables, or may alter a Round
dance, Two-step, or other kind of secular or even religious song. He
may also buy, trade, or "steal" a song from another tribe and modify
it according to the standards of his own tribe's style. No matter how
the song is composed, the composer is limited to a specific song
pattern to which his creative or adaptive impulses must conform.
This conformity must not be viewed as so strict, though, that the
composer may not impose individual style on his compositions.
Individual style plays an important role in diffusion because many
songs are carried off the reservations by a single person. This hap-
pens frequently today with the relocation of individuals off the
reservation areas. The individual singing his tribe's songs or performing its dances in a remote area where his tribesmen are not
present to criticize may feel additional freedom in improvising on
his tribe's traditional music. It must also be noted that individuals
who carry songs from reservations to the urban communities are in
some cases not recognized singers in their own communities. This
would, it seems, have a strong bearing on the diffusion of music,
since in many cases, the carrier, or prime source of diffusion, may
not be a reliable singer according to his own tribe's standards.

MORPHOLOGY AND MODIFICATION

As has been stated before, it is necessary to understand the morphology of the song in order to understand how it is modified in diffusion. If songs retained their original characteristics, tracing the diffusion would be simple; but unfortunately, this is not the case. There is

a great deal of hope for comparative musicologists to salvage existing materials because the melodic and rhythmic components of the song undergo far less change than the style and presentation of the song in a new environment.

The performance of War dance songs generally falls into the classification known as the "incomplete repetition" type, indicating that in each song there are two basic sections, and that the second section is an abbreviated form of the first.

While this serves as a general classification, in order to be specific as to how and why songs change, we must divide the standard War dance song into six parts. These will be described, noting what kind of change (if any) occurs in each as the songs diffuse.

The Introduction or Lead

This is an introductory phrase sung by one man. It has three functions: to identify the song for the other singers, to establish the pitch in the first rendition, and to indicate to the singers that the leader wants to repeat the song.

In some types of diffusion, the lead remains intact. In others, the lead may be lengthened, shortened, raised, lowered, or replaced. In the northern style it is sung more lyrically than in the southern, using open vowel sounds with little enunciation of vocables. In the Southern Plains there is a greater enunciation of vocables, probably due to the lowering of the register. In the classic style, especially among the Lakota, Blackfeet, Cree, and Cheyenne, one hears a number of accented notes resembling shouts or yelps in the lead. The lead is the portion of the song most likely to be modified in any kind of diffusion.

The Second

This is simply a repeat of the lead by the rest of the group. In the northern and classic style, the second interrupts the lead line. On the Southern Plains there is more often a slight pause between the lead and the second. The second usually occurs at a specific point in the lead; however, on the Northern Plains it may appear to overlap almost simultaneously once the first rendition of the song has been sung.

The Chorus

This portion of the song immediately follows the lead and second, and is sung by the entire group. The melody and vocables of the chorus are different in each song. In diffusion, there is less modification of the chorus than of any other section of the song. A good variation to this is found in the northern-style songs, which have hesitations in the chorus that singers outside the style area find difficult to duplicate. It should be noted that it is in this section of the song that female singers join in.

The First Ending

This is a standard section of the War dance song which undergoes little or no modification. Like the chorus, it is sung by the entire group, and signals the halfway point in the song. In addition to the melody, the vocables are somewhat standardized, but may change in diffusion. They may be generally written:

we yo he ye he ye o-oi.

The first ending is sung to the accompaniment of seven beats of the drum. In diffusion, the volume and style of drumming may change.

While in this section there is no particular accenting in the northern or classic style, in Oklahoma the singers play the drum in duple accents, beginning with the last beats of the first ending and continuing through the next part of the song. These beats are called middle beats, or honor beats, and cue the dancers to perform a particular variation in their dance movements in which they slightly bow in the direction of the drum. In the Southern Plains there are usually three accented duple beats.

The women's voices trail off behind the men's in the first ending.

The first four sections are sung in vocables.

The Repeat Chorus

As its name implies, this is simply another rendition of the chorus, but this time without the lead and second. It is sung by the group, including the women.

In Oklahoma, the accented duple beats introduce the repeat

chorus (usually two of them coupled with the third held over from the first ending), but in the Northern Plains they occur in the middle of the repeat chorus. Here we find four or five duple accented beats, though more may be added spontaneously. Generally the volume of the drum decreases at the beginning of the repeat chorus and builds up to fortissimo near the end.

It is in the repeat chorus that words are sometimes used. Interspersed between the words are vocables which are inserted to make the lyrics of the repeat chorus correspond with the vocables of the chorus in time value. This is done somewhat to avoid distorting the words, though some word distortion does exist.

When songs are learned by tribes speaking different languages, the words are dropped and the vocables originally appearing in the chorus are sung in the repeat chorus.

The Final Ending

This section corresponds to the *first ending* with the exception of the last vocable, which changes from *o-oi* to *yo.* It signals the end of one complete song. The seven beats which accompany the final ending normally get progressively louder. The final ending signals the dancers to stop dancing on the last beat.

CONTINUATION OF SONG

During the course of a dance the complete song is repeated over and over, the number of renditions being determined by regional or tribal taste. The number of times the song is sung for a complete dance, as well as other vocal and percussive techniques, change from one region to the next.

Generally, the songs are sung more times through in the north. Some songs may be repeated as many as 20 times. In the south, three or four times is normal. Classic songs tend to be sung a fixed number of times (for example, four times through among the Lakota).

In all areas the several renditions of the song are followed by a "tail," or encore. Among classic Oklahoma songs, the tail is simply one rendition of the repeat chorus and final ending. It is usually separated from the last song by a short pause. On the Northern

Plains, the tail begins with the repeat chorus but, rather than stopping, continues again for another complete song (a total of one and a half songs).

The continuation of song is governed by the lead singer, and in some cases, especially in the north, by a whistle man, a dancer who blows his whistle over the heads of the singers if he wishes them to continue the song. Normally when the first song is nearing the end, the leader begins to sing the lead again while the rest of the group is singing the final ending. This interruption of the group by the leader varies somewhat in different areas. In classic songs there is a definite clash between the voice of the leader and that of the group. This is also more or less true in Oklahoma. In the north, however, the leader may wait until the last two or three beats before the last vocable to begin the lead.

In continuing from the first song to the next, the leader may want to increase the pitch and tempo. The pitch is simply sung higher by the leader without any signal, but if the tempo is to be increased, the leader usually plays a series of accented duple beats right before he begins his lead line. In playing the duple beats he picks up the tempo.

Normally the tempo remains continuous after it has been increased one time, although on the Northern Plains there is a feeling of a slight ritard after the middle beats in the repeat chorus are played.

While it is difficult to generalize about all the music and dance of such a vast area as the Northern and Southern Plains, some general statements can be made about the diffusion of War dance, to which I turn in the next chapter. It must be noted that in the diffusion of music, it is the style and presentation of the War dance that are modified to a greater degree than the actual melodic and rhythmic structure of the song. This modification is governed by the tribe, the style area, and the culture area, until it reaches another culture area where it loses its function as a War dance but may obtain new functions.

In summary, the War dance song has an established morphology which may be divided into six parts. These six parts are affected by the diffusion process and take on the style of its adaptors as it shifts through the tribal, stylistic, and cultural subdivisions.

While there is a general southward song movement on the Plains, because of the Indian's adaptation to modern forms of transportation and communications, the War dance song is difficult to trace with accuracy. The general cradle of creativity seems to lie on the Northern Plains, but a great deal of comparative material does not exist to corroborate where and when the songs originate.

Chapter 4

Music in Motion

In order to understand the manner in which song and dance move from one tribe to the next, sometimes undergoing radical change, I would like to underscore a fundamental distinction between tribalism and intertribalism.[1] Tribal music and dance are always traditional in structure and function, that is, they are associated with one tribal origin. Intertribal music and dance are always traditional in structure but not always so in function. Tribalism deals with a classification of things; intertribalism deals with a classification of processes. Tribalism and intertribalism occur in a dialectical relationship. They are essentially two systems operating coterminously; individuals may participate in both systems. In the past we have regarded them as a single system, leading to our inability to explain the persistence of tribal music and dance, and our exaggeration of the importance of assimilation of tribal traits.

Tribal music and dance represent historical continuity. There is, of course, historical change within each tribe, but the rate of change is slower than in intertribal music and dance exchange, which represents rapid trait diffusion. Tribal music and dance may persist for decades or even centuries. Intertribal music and dance change almost annually. The relationship between the two is dynamic; intertribal changes reflect and synthesize tribal changes. The two systems seem to exhibit the characteristics of an inverse proportionality: the more rapid the change at the intertribal level, the more constant the continuity at the tribal level. The goals of the two systems are quite distinct. Tribalism reinforces ethnic identity, and relates music and dance to other social and cultural categories which are meaningful within individual tribes. Intertribal music and dance reinforce American Indian identity at a higher level where this identity is directly threatened by non-Indian influences. The two systems often operate in the same arena.

Thus at northern powwows, the announcer distinguishes between traditional and "intertribal" dances and songs. The structure and function of the songs are often identical, for example, the War dance of intertribalism and the Omaha dance of Lakota tradition. The distinction, however, is not structural but conceptual and classificatory. We find that at the same time intertribal events burgeoned during the mid-1950s, on the Southern Plains there was a "revitalization" of the Ponca Hethuska and Osage Helushka societies, the Black Legging Society of the Kiowa and Kiowa-Apache, and the Gourd dance "clan" among the western Oklahoma tribes. On the Northern Plains, at the same time Southern Plains dance style was beginning to inundate the South Dakota reservations, we find a renewed interest among the Pine Ridge Lakota and North Dakota Plains Ojibwa in the immolative form of the Sun dance.

Tribal music and dance are of enormous quantity and would require massive collaboration in order adequately to describe and analyze tribal variation. Intertribal music performance, however, is more limited. The essential feature of intertribalism is that its components—music, dance, and material culture—diffuse rapidly not only throughout the whole Plains area but also beyond it. There are essentially three methods of diffusion which generate four types of diffusion models. Music and dance diffuse through (1) direct contact, where members of one tribe learn music and dance forms from direct observation of members of another tribe; (2) stimulus diffusion, where musical and dance concepts of one tribe give rise to similar concepts in other tribes based largely on memory but not on conscious efforts to learn the music or dance form (for example, the Snake dance of the western Oklahoma tribes, which may be Southwest or Southeast in origin),[2] and (3) mechanical diffusion, in which modern recorders and cameras aid in the diffusion of music from one reservation to the next, or snapshots, journal photographs, or films provide inspiration for designing dance costumes which have lost currency for several generations.

Standing on the Prairie, also known as John Grant, Iowa. *Photo by DeLancey Gill, January 1900, Iowa Reservation, Oklahoma. Courtesy of Smithsonian Office of Anthropology, Bureau of American Ethnology Collection.*

Dog Chief, also known as Simond Adams, Pawnee. *Photo taken prior to 1929. Courtesy of Smithsonian Office of Anthropology, Bureau of American Ethnology Collection.*

TYPES AND METHODS OF DIFFUSION

Four types of diffusion exist.

Intratribal Diffusion

In this category, the War dance song is so tribalized through consistent use of word-songs, or unusual tribal variations of the song structure, that while it is widely distributed throughout the districts or linguistic community, it rarely leaves the reservation. Although it is thus restricted, the War song may be modified within the reservation boundaries. The most common way is by changing the words. Because of the interrelationship between vocable and language, this kind of modification may have an effect on the vocable structure. However changed, the War dance song retains its true tribal identity and significance as a tribal function. A good example of intratribal diffusion is found among the Lakota of North and South Dakota, which together form a linguistic community. A Lakota song which originates on the Pine Ridge reservation, while retaining its incipient melody and rhythmic structure, may well receive a new set of words as it moves through the Rosebud, Cheyenne River, and Standing Rock reservations.

Most often, the songs within this category are sung in the "classic" tribal style.

Homostylic Diffusion

As the name indicates, diffusion of songs in this category is limited by the style in which they are sung. Therefore, songs sung in the "northern style" may diffuse rapidly through the Lakota, Cree, Blackfeet, and Three Affiliated Tribes but do not leave the north. They are most often composed of vocables only, and retain the characteristic northern voice, drum style, and, most important, the extremely high pitch. Some classic songs may also be included in this category; however, in diffusion, words are, for obvious reasons, replaced by vocables.

In this category, there is more freedom of adapting Round dance and other secular songs into War dance songs, but there is little or no modification of War dance songs themselves.

Intracultural Diffusion

In this category, we find War dance songs which have broken through the homostylic barrier but remain geographically and functionally within their related cultural area. Northern-style songs infiltrate the Southern Plains (but the reverse is not as pronounced) and in the transition undergo a series of modifications affecting the pitch, tempo, vocable, and drum technique. These specific changes will be noted further along.

There are less "classic"-style songs found in this category; and all songs contain vocables. In essence they, coupled with some songs of the homostylic type, form the nucleus of intertribal music.

The tenuous line which separates the homostylic and the intracultural categories may well be based on the singer's ability to reproduce the exotic sound, or to sing in ranges and play in tempos which are incongruous to his normal range and playing ability, or possibly he finds songs of other styles incompatible with his opinion of esthetic value. This is a matter of conjecture which warrants further investigation and analysis.

Transcultural Diffusion

In this type of diffusion, brought on in recent times through the Indian's adaptation to modern transportation and communications, the War dance song may well transmigrate beyond its cultural delineations. In the process it is not only severely modified—sometimes beyond recognition—but also ceases to exist as a true War dance song. While it loses its original function, it may acquire new functional responsibilities.

The difference, then, between intracultural and transcultural diffusion is that in the latter category the song ceases to function in that capacity for which it was originally composed.

In the case of diffusion of War dance songs into urban areas of Indian relocation, the difference between these two categories may be confusing. When the song leaves its original environment, if its function is still retained, it is still intracultural (or possibly even intratribal or homostylic). To illustrate, let us imagine that a War dance song, originally composed by Lakota in South Dakota, diffuses to the American Indian Center in Chicago. The song will retain the characteristics of an intratribally or homostylically diffused song. If the Lakota singers leave the Center to return to the reservation, the melody may very well linger on—to be sung by Winnebagos, Chippewa, or other tribes who are also relocated in Chicago. At this point the song will lose its words, and automatically fall out of the intratribal category, but may well stay in the homostylic category if the new singers favor the northern or classic Lakota style. Since the song still retains its form and is sung for War dancing, it is also intracultural. In essence, not only the song but the entire Plains culture has diffused to Chicago. Only when this same song, under scrutiny by a lonely Navajo or Mohawk, leaves the Center and goes back to Arizona or New York, where it is sung as a "Western Indian song" for the amusement of non-Plains listeners, does it truly become transcultural. At this juncture the song has lost its words, usually its form, and always its original purpose.

PROCESS OF DIFFUSION

The methods and channels through which the War dance song is diffused are best understood if we begin at the point where the song is composed.

From inception, the song, if composed on a reservation, moves intratribally in the following way:

1. The composer teaches the new song to another individual or his song group. This is an educative process effected through repetition.

2. Alternatively, the composer may save the new song and introduce it at a celebration or powwow. As he sings the song once or twice through, his group learns on the spot. After completing steps 1 and/or 2, the song is then established.

3. The song group travels from district to district on the reservation, introducing the song. Or a second group assimilates the song and in turn introduces it at other district celebrations. In a short time, the song makes the reservation circuit of dances.

4. The composer and his group, or another group, attend a dance on a neighboring reservation and introduce the song, whereby

through step 3 it is diffused throughout the new reservation, and so on ad infinitum.

Steps 1 and 2, given that the song is composed on a reservation and has the characteristics of a tribal song, are the only reliable steps. Once the song has been introduced to the public, a number of variables make it unpredictable as to how and in what direction the song will diffuse. This is especially true on the Southern Plains, where there is an absence of reservations.

Today there is more and more travel between reservations, and songs may diffuse rapidly in all directions after they are composed. There is a general tendency for songs to diffuse southward, as has been noted. Both Northern and Southern Plains songs also go east and west to urban areas. In addition, more and more singers have acquired tape recorders and to some degree exchange songs by mail. And, of course, there is that ever present phenomenon relative to Indian music that makes it impossible to prevent an Indian singer from "catching" a song. Whether he makes it a point to learn a new song or not, he will invariably return home from a dance to find himself singing a song he unconsciously "learned" several days past. How accurately he remembers it and passes it on to other singers greatly accounts for the modification of songs in the process of diffusion.

The relationship between diffusion models is shown in Table 2.

To better understand the diffusion of music and dance within the Plains area, it is perhaps beneficial to make still another distinction between music and dance music.

This higher level of distinction deals with universals of Plains music and dance. Of essential importance (here I borrow somewhat from the arguments of religionists over the primacy of myth and ritual,[3] except on firmer and more empirical grounds), I categorically state that music is primary and dance is secondary. Music is not necessarily older than dance, but empirically the two categories of expressive culture occupy asymmetrical positions in all Plains (if not all) tribes. The outstanding distinction is that music, even dance music, may be performed without dance accompaniment, but dance can never be performed without proper musical accompani-

Table 2 Diffusion Models

Type	Environment	Example[a]
1. Intratribal	tradition	A1, A1b, etc.
		A2, A2b, etc.
		3a
		A4a, A4b, etc.
		B1a, B1b, etc.
		B2a, B2b, etc.
2. Homostylic	region	A1, A2, A3, A4
		B1, B2
3. Geocultural	Northern Plains	A
	Southern Plains	B
4. Intracultural	Plains culture area	AB
5. Transcultural	Extraculture area(s)	ABC1a, etc.[b]

[a]See Table 1.
[b]Where *C* stands for another tradition outside the Plains area.

ment. This distinction, I believe, has many implications which may be applicable to general theories of music and dance.

The distinction allows one to disregard, at least temporarily, that rather overworked anthropological notion that all American Indian music and dance is "functional." Of course, if everything is functional, the term "functional" itself is hardly significant in attempting to explain or analyze any sociocultural category. To limit one's discourse to the function of music and dance is to guarantee that these domains will never be associated with others or undergo change. In the past, music and dance have been regarded as functional with respect to each other, but to hardly anything else. I of course recognize that music also has been regarded as functionally related to other cultural categories (for example, work songs, religious songs, and riding songs), but the relationships between these categories have never been studied in the larger context (such as politics, economics, kinship, etc.).

Given the primacy of music over dance, I believe anthropologists and ethnomusicologists can begin studying the two categories more rewardingly. For example, at the level of the relationships between song and dance, we find music more bound to cultural or tribal context. In Oklahoma, a number of specialty dances have been imported from other tribes: the Snake dance, done in conjunction with the Buffalo dance; the Stomp dance, from the Southeast (and eastern Oklahoma); the Hoop dance and Eagle dance from the Southwest.[4] However, songs composed by the original owners of these dances have not been imported—new or traditional songs from the recipient tribe have been adapted and used. Even within the context of esoteric dance form, such as the War dance or Round dance, Northern and Southern Plains variations are marked by a similar variation in song style. Perhaps the best examples of contrast in song style (but not the structure of the song, which is identical) are drum tempo and duration. Categorically—and this is a subject critically evaluated by American Indian singers and dancers—in the north, War dance songs are slower and longer; in the south, they are faster and shorter.

Again looking at the distinction between music and dance, and remembering the former's primacy, music is more flexible, more open to improvisation, elaboration, and individual style than dance. A single musical concept, whether melodic or textual, may be structured to accommodate a variety of musical genres. Among the Lakota, a love song may be converted into a dance song or a flageolet melody. The same text of the love song may be used in Omaha or Round dance songs. A ritual song may be based on a popular dance melody. There seems no end to the number of variations a single musical idea may generate. On the other hand, dance patterns are rather static. Once incorporated into the choreographic inventory of the tribe or region, dances rarely undergo structural changes—they persist in both structure and function over long periods of time.

Chapter 5

The Powwow

In the Plains reservation period, beginning in the late 1870s, the most notable feature with respect to continuity and change in music and dance forms is the relative stability of tribal locations. Relative isolation on the Northern Plains contrasts with the fluid interaction between Indian tribes and non-Indian communities in the Southern Plains, particularly since the 1920s, when reservations (except for the Osage) were abolished in Oklahoma.

Despite the early belief that Indian cultures were dying out, a number of events occurred to strengthen rather than weaken Indian values, particularly music and dance. First, World War I—which took place only 25 years after the Wounded Knee Massacre—induced young American Indian men to volunteer for military service. The effect this had on native culture was to guarantee that many social institutions would maintain a sense of relevancy despite their anticipated degeneration and obsolescence. American Indians in fact had an opportunity to become "warriors" again, thus permitting songs and dances related to war to retain a function within each of the Plains societies. Not enough time elapsed for these cultural institutions to die out. In fact, there was a decided need for further institutions, which were to become the nucleus of modern intertribal events such as the powwow.[1]

Sixteen years after the end of World War I, the Indian Reorganization Act was passed, which gave positive sanction to Indianness. Interestingly enough, among some Northern Plains tribes this policy gave rise to reinstituting many tribal functions which had earlier been prohibited—specifically, the Sun dance.

Within only seven years of the Indian Reorganization Act, World War II broke out, and again American Indians entered military service. This has naively been interpreted solely as a mark of "patriotism" on the part of American Indians (Daniels 1970). My own interpretation of the effects of World Wars I and II and, to a lesser extent, Korea and Vietnam, is that they gave American Indians the opportunity to reinforce cultural institutions that might have become dysfunctional. Indian soldiers who participated were regarded as heroes by their people and, in accordance with tribal custom, were publicly acknowledged through songs, dances, and giveaways.

More recently, certain federal programs have tended to bolster Indianness. Federal grants available to Indian cultural and bilingual programs are numerous, and in many cases, federal funds have supported music and dance events in a way they have never been supported before.

Because music and dance are so visible, they have often served as indices of contemporary directions in American Indian cultural interests. We can cite 1955, the date of James H. Howard's seminal article on Oklahoma powwows, as the beginning of increased interest in the exchange of traits between tribes, which anthropologists in particular were quick to accept as "Pan-Indianism."[2] In Chapter 7 I argue that the amalgamation of musical and dance traits in Oklahoma does not readily hold for other parts of the Plains. Oklahoma was in fact ripe for an extensive exchange of tribal customs related to music and dance, despite the fact that tribalism in Oklahoma also continued.

There has always been a distinction between that which is tribal and that which is intertribal even in the so-called cradle of "Pan-Indianism." I believe that intertribal events have tended to serve as a cultural halfway house between American Indian and white societies. For many tribes (especially the Ponca and the Kiowa) "Pan-Indianism," once defined as "an attempt to create a new ethnic group, the American Indian" (Thomas 1965:75), did not hinder the reconstitution of tribal customs. As Lurie has pointed out (1965), many Indians dislike the anthropologists' term "Pan-Indianism," arguing that powwows and the Native American Church are cases of mutual borrowing and enrichment of the cultures of different tribes.

Many anthropologists have been quick to apply Howard's definition to all tribes. But in emphasizing the postulated homogeneity of "Pan-Indianism," they have failed to recognize tribal distinctiveness.

Table 3 provides a quick reference to contemporary Plains events, their locations, dates, and, where known, the date of the origin of the specific event. These are listed alphabetically by tribe. The dates and locations are apt to change annually.

The date of origin refers to the year in which the tribe in question consciously began to "count" its annual events: it does not necessarily mean that this was the year the event was introduced. In most cases, powwows were going on a long time before the listed date of origin. All of the events listed are presumed to be held annually.

Most of the principal Plains tribes sponsor one or more events, mostly in the summer months. Table 3 does not document urban events, which are held during the winter in schools, gymnasiums, church basements, American Indian centers, and other locations with some frequency, ranging from weekly to monthly. Ad hoc secular and ritual events are not counted.

Earlier, in speaking of analytical distinctions, I avoided the age-old dichotomy between religious and secular music and dance, because at the level of structure there is little difference between songs performed for religious events and for secular ones. The striking difference between them is contextual rather than structural. In some cases, religious songs are sung for secular events, and vice versa. Thus, a sacred song may open a powwow, and a secular song may be sung for the amusement of supernatural spirits at a religious meeting.

The nature of Plains Indian music and dance style is still governed initially by geocultural boundaries. Tribal music is composed every year, or as needed in the case of songs learned in the vision quest and Native American Church ceremonies. Whether music strictly for tribal performance is produced more or less frequently than music for intertribal events is not known: I believe that both catego-

Table 3 Contemporary Plains Events

Tribe	Event	Location	Time	Origin
		TRIBAL		
Arapahoe (Northern)	Sun Dance	Arapaho, Ethete WY	July	
	Arapaho Powwow	Ethete WY	July	
	Labor Day Powwow	Ethete WY	Sept.	
Arapaho (Southern)	Gourd Dance	Colony OK	June, Sept.	
	Arapaho Powwow	Canton OK	Aug.	
Assiniboine-Sioux	Wolf Point Stampede	Wolf Point MT	July	
	Assiniboine Encampment	Poplar MT	Aug.	
Blackfeet	Blackfeet Indian Rodeo	Browning MT	July	
	Blackfeet Indian Days	Cluny, Alberta	July	
	North American Indian Days	Browning MT	July	
Caddo	Caddo Powwow	Binger, Gracemont OK	June, Sept.	1927
Cheyenne (Northern)	Cheyenne Sun Dance	Lame Deer MT	July	
	Northern Cheyenne Powwow	Lame Deer MT	July	
	Cheyenne Fair	Lame Deer MT	Aug.	
Cheyenne (Southern)	Cheyenne Powwow	El Reno OK	June	
	Cheyenne-Arapaho Powwow	Clinton OK	June	
	Cheyenne Sun Dance	Seiling OK	—	
Comanche	Comanche Powwow	Walters OK	July	
Cree (Plains)	Cree Sun Dance	Box Elder MT	June	

Table 3 *Continued*

Tribe	Event	Location	Time	Origin
Crow	Crow Sun Dance	Lodge Grass MT	June	
	Crow Fair	Crow Agency MT	Aug.	
	Crow Indian Powwow	Hardin MT	Aug.	
Gros Ventre	Powwow	Harlem MT	July	
Sioux				
Cheyenne River	Sun Dance	Eagle Butte SD	Aug.	
	Powwow	Red Scaffold SD	Aug.	
	Powwow	Eagle Butte SD	Sept.	
Devil's Lake	Powwow	Tokio ND	—	
	Rodeo and Powwow	Ft. Totten ND	Sept.	
Standing Buffalo	Grand Sioux Powwow	Ft. Qu'Appelle Saskatchewan	July, Aug.	
Crow Creek	Powwow	Ft. Thompson SD	July, Aug.	
Pine Ridge	Sun Dance	Alternating communities	July, Aug.	
	Powwows	All districts	May, Sept.	
Rosebud	Sun Dance	Spring Creek SD	July, Aug.	
	Powwow	All districts	May–Sept.	
Standing Rock	Powwow	Bullhead, Cannon Ball, Ft. Yates ND	May–Sept.	
Flandreau	Santee Sioux Powwow	Flandreau SD	July	
Three Affiliated Tribes	Three Affiliated Tribes Powwow	New Town ND	July	
	White Shield Powwow	Emmet ND	July	
Iowa	Iowa Powwow	Rulo NE	June	

Tribe	Event	Location	Month	Year
Kiowa	Gourd Clan Dance	Carnegie OK	July	
	Tia-piah Society	Ft. Sill, Lawton OK	July	
	Blackfoot Society	Carnegie OK	Sept.	
	Veterans' Dance	Anadarko OK	Nov.	
Kiowa-Apache	Kiowa-Apache Powwow	Ft. Cobb OK	June, Aug.	
	Kiowa-Apache Blackfoot Society	Ft. Cobb OK	June, Aug.	
Ojibwa (Plains)	Sun Dance	Turtle Mountain ND	June	
	Ojibwa Powwow	Belcourt ND	July	
Omaha	Powwow	Macy NE	—	
Osage	Osage Dance	Hominy OK	June	
	Osage Dance	Pawhuska OK	June	
	Osage Dance	Gray Horse OK	June	
Oto-Missouri	Oto Dance	Perry OK	Sept.	
Pawnee	Pawnee Homecoming	Pawnee OK	July	1946
Piegan	Piegan Indian Days	Alberta	Aug.	
Ponca	Ponca Powwow	White Eagle, Ponca City OK	Aug.	1887
	Ponca Fair	White Eagle OK	Aug.	1953
Quapaw	Quapaw Powwow	Quapaw OK	July	
Sarcee	Sarcee Indian Days	Calgary, Alberta	Aug.	

INTERTRIBAL

	Event	Location	Month	Year
	All American Indian Days	Sheridan WY	June, July	1931
	American Indian Exposition (Originally, Caddo County Fair)	Anadarko OK	July, Aug.	(1922)
	Cheyenne Frontier Days	Cheyenne WY	July	
	Mid-America All Indian Days	Wichita KS	July, Aug.	

ries are represented in fairly equal numbers. Songs related to Sun dances, and other events presumed to be owned or originated by a particular tribe, change little, if at all. However, songs related to sweat lodge use, vision quests, curing rituals, and funeral rites do change—often dramatically—within a traditional structural framework.

Dances may diffuse, but they have rarely been created anew since the turn of the twentieth century. Dances performed in both secular and religious contexts are rather stable, although minor stylistic modifications often occur in both contexts, usually under the direction or influence of individuals who have license to innovate, such as medicine men, War dance competitors, and lead singers.

The major powwow dances performed in a secular context on the Northern Plains are the War dance, Round dance, Rabbit dance, Owl dance, and Stomp dance (the latter not to be confused with the Southern Plains Stomp dance influenced by Southeast tribes). On the Southern Plains, the most popular dances are the War dance, Round dance, Forty-nine, Stomp dance, Two-step, Snake and Buffalo dance, and Gourd dance (for the latter, see Howard 1976). I have provided descriptions for most of the others (Powers 1961a, 1962a, 1962b, 1966a, 1968).

Dances and costume styles are set mainly by participants in War dance competition, which has existed on the Southern Plains since about 1900. Competition is relatively new on the Northern Plains; again, 1955 seems a reasonable historical marker. Since 1955, Oklahoma regulations for War dance competition—with minor modifications—have been adopted in the Northern Plains. Today, these events are expanding both in types of competitions (e.g., War dance, Fancy, Traditional, women's, youths', children's) and in frequency. The rules which originally governed Oklahoma War dance competitions (e.g., dancing in time with the song and drum, and ending on the last beat of the drum) hold for the Northern Plains. However, the competitions are marked by long, extended songs on the Northern Plains and by relatively short ones on the Southern Plains.

The stakes are also getting higher in both areas.[3] The increased emphasis on competition, underscored by a general agreement that powwows with high stakes attract the best dancers and are most successful, has had some deleterious effects. Personal and social

Comanche war dancers wearing typical fancy dance costumes of the 1950s and 1960s. The man on the far right carrying the eagle wing fan is champion war dancer, George "Woogie" Watchetaker. *Courtesy of Bureau of Indian Affairs.*

relations have been challenged because of the highly competitive nature of some powwows. My own interpretation is that music and dance culture is threatened by such attacks on solidarity, and the competitions will slowly be eliminated.[4]

Composition and performance of music are still in the purview of men, although women participate much more today, particularly in dance. In the late 1960s, women's dance style in Oklahoma differed strikingly from that in the Northern Plains, but the difference is fading. This has come about largely because of the wide diffusion of intertribal events. Before 1950, the term "powwow" was used only on the Southern Plains; today, it is commonly used to identify the most popular Plains event—Plains in origin and influence—which is mainly secular in context. The powwow is perhaps the event to which the term "Pan-Indianism" has been applied more than any other. But powwows are not identical in structure and content as one moves from the Northern to the Southern Plains. However, they are similar enough that dancers from one area may participate in the other and understand the local rules and regulations.

Powwows occur frequently during the summer so that interested parties (both Indians and anthropologists!) may travel from one to the next on what is called the "powwow circuit." Powwows include singing, dancing, giveaways, specialty dances, and feasts. Participants camp out around a circular arbor for a weekend or a week; dance during the afternoon and evening; and leave with enough time to reach the next powwow several miles, or hundreds of miles, away.

Before 1955, the term "War dance" had not reached the Northern Plains, where the same general style and pattern of dance was called by tribal names: Omaha dance, Hot dance, Chicken dance, Wolf dance, and so on (and still is, when speaking the native language). At this time no particular War dance style dominated the Northern Plains, although there were regional variations. In the Southern Plains, however, there was a sharp distinction between the style of the northern Oklahoma tribes (the Ponca, Pawnee, Oto-Missouri, Osage, and Kansa), which was called "Straight" dancing, and the style of the central Oklahoma tribes (Comanche, Kiowa, Apache, Cheyenne, and Arapaho), most of whom performed "Fancy" dancing. The two styles were reflected in drum type and tempo (Straight dancing was slower and dignified; Fancy dancing, fast and furious), and the dance costume. Fancy dancers wore feathered costumes; Straight dancers wore tailored costumes with feathers only in their headdresses. The two dance styles were distinct enough that separate competitions were held in both categories. Women's dance costumes varied on a tribal rather than a regional basis, including two basic costume types: buckskin dresses and cloth dresses. Likewise, contests were held for women on the basis of attire rather than dance style.

The singing style for Fancy dancing, most often heard on the Southern Plains, has been dominated by the Kiowa, Comanche, Cheyenne, and Arapaho, while the Straight dance style has been

Women dancing to an honor song, ca. 1940s. Wolf Creek Community, Pine Ridge. *Courtesy of the Heritage Center, Inc.*

dominated by the Osage and Ponca. Other tribal singers participate in both styles, and both often appear at intertribal events. Good singers can sing in both styles. The singing distinctions are not always very clear except at tribal events, such as Osage war dances or Ponca Hethuska Society dances. A segment of time is often allotted for tribal dances, and other time for intertribal.

Before 1955, regional styles underwent little diffusion. Later, however, the Northern Plains was strongly influenced by the Oklahoma Fancy dance style but not by its singing styles. By the 1960s the trend reversed, and the southernmost reservations on the Northern Plains began to be influenced by what they called the "North Dakota" style in music, dance, and costumes (Howard 1960). By the 1970s, a synthesis had taken place in which we find "South Dakota"-style costumes worn by the Oklahoma Fancy dancers, and the Northern Plains tribes distinguishing between Fancy dancing (which is still essentially North Dakota style rather than Oklahoma) and "Traditional," or what is now called "Straight" dancing, to distinguish traditional South Dakota style from North Dakota and Oklahoma styles.

Intertribal styles change annually, while tribal styles seem to remain nearly constant. Despite an increased interest in Pan-Indianism, it is at the height of intertribal exchange, about 1955, that we find vitalization and acceleration of distinctly tribal institutions, such as the Southern Plains Black Legging Society, Heluska Society, and Gourd dance societies cited earlier. In the Northern Plains, we find a reconstituted Sun dance focused on piercing, which had not been publicly performed since the 1880s. As a result of this survey, culminating in the summer of 1987, we conclude that the major substance of American Indian music and dance on the Plains remains irrevocably tribal.

Chapter 6

Pan-Indianism versus Pan-Tetonism

Since the late 1940s I have observed and recorded American Indian music and dance in Oklahoma, South Dakota, and many urban Indian centers. I have watched the evolution of the "powwow," and am convinced that Pan-Indianism, by any definition, has sustained a vital American Indian practice. At times this practice has seemed homogeneous across many tribes. At other times a conglomerate of traits has served to revive an individual tribal past. But whether tribalistic or Pan-Indianistic, the complex is irrefutably "Indian."

Today we are witnessing a cultural metamorphosis which may nationalize the American Indian, but the degree to which nationalization can replace tribal identity is little known.[1] In the past, what has been suggested as typical Pan-Indian has been basically an aggregate of Pan-Plains cultural elements. Thomas (1965:77) states:

> . . . It is on the Plains that we find the historic roots of modern Pan-Indianism. The horse not only enabled Plains Indians to become extremely mobile in hunting and "warfare," but also increased inter-tribal contacts. Even a sign language developed in the area to provide communication across linguistic boundaries. By the 1800's not only had intensive "warfare" and very mobile hunting developed, but tribes were beginning to ally with one another, camp with one another and inter-marry with one another. Most significant for the later development of Pan-Indianism, the Plains style of life was extremely attractive to tribes on the edges of the Plains area. Plains traits and institutions were spreading to other areas even at the time that Plains Indians were becoming pacified and

settled on reservations. Indeed, the Plains style of life was very at-
tractive to American Indians completely outside of the Plains area.
This is one of the historic sources and causes of what is generally
referred to as "Pan-Indianism" which I am suggesting now is in
some degree an extension of the Plains culture area.

Not only have the music and dance aspects of Pan-Indianism been
treated as an extension of the Plains culture, but most anthropologists have tended to investigate the complex as it flourishes in
Oklahoma (Howard 1955) and in urban America wherever there
are American Indian centers (Lurie 1965). In Oklahoma and in a
number of cities Indians representing a multitude of tribes congregate but are not always conscious of the nature of their unification.

Previous definitions tended to focus on Pan-Indianism in its aggregate form without taking into consideration the many ramifica-
tions of its elements (tribal or non-Indian) which comprise the total
complex. Yet each element of Pan-Indianism can be traced to either
tribal or non-Indian origins. In treating Pan-Indianism as an aggregate, only the results of Pan-Indianism become apparent, and the
causative elements are neglected. Hence, the individuals directly
involved in Pan-Indian events seem to be the recipients of what
might be termed incongruous tribal innovations.

Three questions may be raised. What are the prominent elements
in Oklahoma Pan-Indianism which are alien and incompatible with
well-rooted tribalistic patterns? What form does Pan-Indianism take
in a tribe or division of tribes which are closely related by a common
language and sense of tribal heritage? Where tribal identity is still
strong, particularly on reservations, what elements does a tribe
contribute to Pan-Indianism outside their boundaries? In this chapter I will discuss the various elements of Pan-Indianism as they
appear among a Teton division, the Oglala, and analyze to what extent typical Oklahoma Pan-Indianism affects what might be called
the "Pan-Teton" complex as it is manifested in North and South
Dakota.[2]

THE PAN-TETON COMPLEX

Pan-Tetonism, as used here, is the complex whole shared by seven
Teton tribes with similarities in language, historical relationship,

interpretation of various Plains traits such as the Sun dance, vision quest, and warrior and chief societies. The seven tribes designate themselves as (1) Oglala, "they scatter their own"; (2) Sicangu, "burned thighs," also known as Brule; (3) Mnikowoju, "they plant near the water," also called Mniconjou; (4) Hunkpapa, "end of the horn"; (5) Sihasapa, "black foot"; (6) Itazipcola, "without bows," also called Sans Arc; and (7) Oohe nunpa, "two boilings," also called Two Kettle. Historically the Oglala and Sicangu are referred to as the southern Teton, while the remaining five are known collectively as the Saone, an anglicized spelling of *canona* (Nakota dialect). The origin of this word has been lost, but it refers in some way to "woods." Although linguistically and historically related, the tribes do not have identical traits; in fact, there are differences in Lakota dialect from reservation to reservation, and some disagreement from tribe to tribe as to who was the most important in history, for instance.

Within Pan-Tetonism there are two forces. One is "tradition," which all members of the complex refer to as Lakota. The other is rooted in North Dakota and is referred to by the tribes living in South Dakota as "North Dakota." Both forces have been influenced by Oklahoma Pan-Indianism, especially in the mid-1950s, and it is my contention that, historically, the strongest influences on the Teton tribes have come from within the Pan-Teton complex itself. Hence, the South Dakotans are more directly influenced by that which is "North Dakota" than that which is generally accepted as Pan-Indian. The greatest significance is that, more than ever, today the Pan-Teton group is influencing the larger Pan-Indian complex, in some instances proving even more significant than Oklahoma Pan-Indianism.

To illustrate the connections between Oklahoma Pan-Indianism and Pan-Tetonism, I shall investigate (1) characteristic elements of Oklahoma Pan-Indianism; (2) characteristic elements of Pan-Tetonism; (3) Oklahoma elements found in Pan-Tetonism; (4) Pan-Teton elements found in Oklahoma Pan-Indianism; and (5) the Oglala (survival versus revival).

The Oglala will serve to illustrate Pan-Tetonism, keeping in mind that criteria would change somewhat if a North Dakota tribe were substituted. The specific media for analysis are music and dance, including those customs and paraphernalia which are employed in the performance of music and dance.

CHARACTERISTIC ELEMENTS OF OKLAHOMA PAN-INDIANISM

Following are brief descriptions of those elements which are most constant at Oklahoma "powwows."

Powwow

The "powwow" is the main Pan-Indian celebration. It is a secular event featuring group singing and social dancing by men, women, and children. The elements of the powwow originate both from tribal functions and from non-Indian influences. The concept of today's powwow is a vestige of the Grass dance complex that spread across the Great Plains during the mid-nineteenth century. The powwow in Oklahoma is sponsored by almost all Plains tribes, and may take place on patriotic holidays such as the Kiowa Veterans' Day celebration. Sometimes smaller powwows are held spontaneously. In larger cities, at the local Indian centers many are held on a weekly or monthly basis.

War Dance

The most prominent dance at the powwow is the War dance. While performed by men, women, and children, it is designed primarily for men. The dance is free style and individualistic, although there are common steps and a variety of accepted body movements. The male dancers improvise on a theme; the women perform one basic walking step. In Oklahoma, the dance has two forms: the Fancy War dance, a fast and lively style which is also used for contest dancing; and the Straight dance, a slow, conservative dance. The Fancy War dance has influenced non-Oklahoma Indians across the nation, while the Straight dance (with many customs observed in the original Grass dance) is not popular outside the state.

During the course of a powwow, which may last from one evening to a weekend, the War dance is danced more than any other. In Oklahoma the songs are usually sung in series of four, each song being sung progressively faster, with only a slight pause between them to keep the dancers on the floor.

War Dance Song

This song is sung for the War dance accompaniment. While there are literally hundreds of War dance songs, they all conform to one basic structure (see Chapter 3). In Oklahoma, they are sung without words, only vocables. Many of today's songs have diffused from the north, and there is some indication that Oklahoma musical creativity is diminishing.[3]

The Procession

This is a parade-like dance which usually brings the dancers onto the dance area. One of the most popular songs used is adapted from a Comanche religious song sung without its original words. The procession concept is non-Indian in origin.

The Round Dance

This is the second most popular dance at a powwow, and is performed in a circle by men, women, and children moving clockwise. Sometimes the dancers hold hands or lock arms, but this is not mandatory. The Round dance is different from any other and must not be confused with other dances performed in a circle. When there is no processional, the Round dance is performed first. The name "Welcome dance" is often applied to it in urban centers. Its origin is most often attributed to the Plains "Scalp dance" or other societal dances performed in a circle.

Round Dance Songs

Round dance songs are sung exclusively for the Round dance, and although there are hundreds of them, they, like the War dance songs, conform to a singular pattern easily recognizable by the dancers.

The Forty-nine

The Forty-nine is a social dance for young men and women performed in concentric circles around a group of male singers who beat on a drum or any resonator. It is always performed at night, in mufti, usually in darkness. Owing to frequent drinking by the participants, sometimes followed by drunken brawls, local authorities attempt to prevent Forty-nines whenever possible. The origin of this dance was in Oklahoma and has been described by Feder (1964).

Forty-nine Songs

These songs are sung exclusively for Forty-nines, often without words, although many contain English phrases. They are played faster than Round dance songs but have a similar structure. One has its origin in Kiowa War Travel songs.

Stomp Dance

This dance, one of the few non-Plains elements in Oklahoma Pan-Indianism, is Creek-Seminole in origin, but it has become an integral part of the powwow. The dance is serpentine, like follow-the-leader; its songs are antiphonal and vary, depending on the repertory of the leader. Both men and women participate. The women wear turtle shell or milk can "shakers" strapped below their knees. This provides the only accompaniment. The Creek-Seminole Stomp dance has been described by Howard (1965a); the Iroquois version, by Kurath (1964). It fits in well as a competitor of the Forty-nine. At some powwows both dances occur simultaneously a few yards apart. The young people run back and forth from one dance to another, forming concentric circles at the Forty-nine drum or attaching themselves to the tail of the Stomp dance line.

Contests

The most popular is the Fancy War dance contest, which is divided into age groups—junior and senior. The rules of the contest generally state that the dancers (who are judged on an individual or "championship" basis) must keep in time with the music, stop on precisely the last beat of the drum, and not drop any article of costuming. The songs for the Fancy War dance contest are extremely fast and are normally sung through twice without a coda. There are also contests in Straight dancing and miscellaneous specialty dances. Contests of these types are non-Indian in origin.

Powwow Princess

At each of the larger Pan-Indian powwows, a powwow princess representing her tribe and/or the celebration itself is chosen. Prerequisites match those of most non-Indian beauty contests, but she must (1) have a certain percentage of Indian blood and (2) be dressed in the traditional costume of her tribe. Upon being invested as powwow princess, she usually leads the Round dance and Two-step with the head dancer.

Head Dancer

A head dancer is usually a young Fancy dancer and championship War dancer whose duty it is to lead (be the first to dance) each War dance. No other dancer may begin until the head dancer is on the floor. At larger celebrations more than one may be chosen, and frequently females are chosen as head lady dancer.

Tail Dancer

Tail dancers are found only in conjunction with Straight dance rules and are a vestige of a Grass dance custom.

Whip Dancer

Whip dancers are used only in conjunction with Straight dancing or secular societal functions. The whip is symbolically used to command someone to dance and is a vestige of the original Grass dance.

Female War Dancers

There are a handful of young women who dress in the manner of young men and dance the War dances with equally virile movements. This appears to have originated in Oklahoma.

Giveaway

The custom of giving away to friends or in honor of someone, usually a deceased relative, is observed in Oklahoma and usually takes place between War dances and other parts of the program. This custom is observed by all Plains tribes, but the formality of the giveaway has its genesis in the Grass dance complex.

Feast

At some powwows, food is given away to anybody who attends. This is also a standard Pan-Plains trait.

Committee

Each powwow has a committee which oversees all arrangements, including the selection of the head dancers, singers, master of ceremonies, and other miscellaneous details. The announcements at Oklahoma powwows are made in English; however, upon occasion an old man may be asked to give an invocation in his tribal language. The committee is a vestige of the various men's societies which alternated as sponsors.

Flag Song

Most tribes have their own Flag songs, which supplant the National Anthem at powwow functions. Most good singers know the Flag songs of other tribes. They are usually sung with vocables only; however, each song has a set of words which are sung at purely tribal functions. The Flag song is of non-Indian origin and became one of the patriotic elements initiated by Indian participation in World War I.

Specials

There are a number of dances called "specials" that are performed in conjunction with Pan-Indian powwows. They are usually show numbers, although some are purely social dances in which all participate. Normally the dances listed below are performed only once a day (or evening), whereas the dances mentioned above are performed in succession throughout the day and night. The most frequent dances are the following:

1. Two-step. A partner dance in which men and women grasp in the skater's position and shuffle forward. Its origin is non-Indian, a simulated waltz first observed at Army posts.

2. Snake and Buffalo. A group dance for men and women. Actually they are two dances performed in succession, as if they were one. The Snake dance is a follow-the-leader dance. The first man in line is the head of the snake, and the last man is the tail. The Buffalo dance is originally a Plains dance—probably Comanche—in which the dancers imitate the movements of the buffalo.

3. Spear and Shield dance. A typical show dance in which two men, or several groups of two, carrying spears and shields pretend to fight each other. It was originated purely for show.

4. Hoop dance. Another spectacular show dance in which a solo dancer manipulates one or more hoops over and about his body. Sometimes there are Hoop dance contests. The origin is debatable. The greatest exponents are the Pueblos; however, dancers on the Northern Plains carried similar hoops in dream society functions.

Each of the above except the Hoop dance has its own particular songs which are not interchangeable with any other. The Hoop dance is usually accompanied by a standard War dance song.

Men's Costumes

Howard (1965b) has described the Fancy War dance costume of the Oklahoma male. The style of this costume is found nearly everywhere Pan-Indian dancers celebrate. There are no tribal differences. It basically consists of a porcupine and deer tail headdress, beaded aprons, cuffs, armbands, belt, galluses, moccasins, choker, and characteristic neck and tail feathers called "bustles." The Oklahoma costume is highly tailored by non-Indian standards, featuring matched beadwork and featherwork.

Women's Costumes

Unlike the men, the Oklahoma women have no typical Pan-Indian costume. Each costume represents the woman's tribal clothing. At some functions, however, women wear clothing of non-Indian manufacture augmented with a shawl or blanket over the shoulders if not in costume, and carried folded over one arm if in costume.

Peyote Paraphernalia

Even though the Oklahoma Pan-Indian powwows are of a secular nature, certain religious items connected with Peyotism are carried by male and female dancers. These include fans, silverwork accessories, blankets, and sashes. Wearing Peyote paraphernalia does not necessarily indicate that the dancer is a Peyotist.

Patriotic Organizations

A highlight of many Pan-Indian powwows is the presence of various Indian patriotic organizations, such as the War Mothers Club, Veterans of Foreign Wars, and American Legion. Occasionally dances are either sponsored by them or given in their behalf.

CHARACTERISTIC ELEMENTS OF PAN-TETONISM

The elements of Oklahoma Pan-Indianism described above have infiltrated Pine Ridge, but the Oglala have not completely forsaken tribal customs for the "new" Indianism. There are elements which parallel each other but, in the main, Pan-Indianism simply provides a framework for specific tribal celebrations, in which the dances and songs are generally related to earlier tribal functions.

To illustrate, let us compare typical Oglala elements with those found in Oklahoma:

Powwow

This term was used commonly to denote what was originally called *wowaci,* or *wacipi,* both nouns signifying "dance," between the 1950s and 1970s. The older Lakota term is popular again. When speaking Lakota, the traditional term is always used in preference to "powwow." This is not true in other instances when a common English word replaces a Lakota equivalent.

War Dance

These words are becoming popular. However, in Lakota the general term is *Omaha wacipi,* "Omaha dance," thus called because the Oglala received the older Grass dance from the Omaha tribe. The traditional Omaha dance of the Oglala closely resembles the Oklahoma Straight dance but is less conservative in movement. In the mid-1950s the Oklahoma style of War dancing became popular on the Pine Ridge reservation along with the Oklahoma Fancy dance costumes. In the 1960s many Oglala adapted the North Dakota style, in both dance and costume. More recently, beginning in the 1970s, the Oglala have created what some call "New Sioux" (Theisz 1974).

To fully appreciate the nuances of War dancing, it is necessary to discuss just what is meant by "style" and what constitutes "popular styles."

In all Pan-Indian War dancing, whether in Oklahoma, in urban areas, or on reservations, there are primary styles of War dancing, each having secondary, or more, substyles discernible to the trained eye.

Dancers at Pine Ridge, ca. 1960. *Courtesy of the Heritage Center, Inc.*

Style in dancing does not apply only to certain accepted dance patterns, choreography, or standardized steps, postures, and directional movements. It also reveals a certain attitude. Ultimately, the "good" dancer is judged by other dancers and the general viewing public on his ability to combine an accepted style with his personal attitude, which ultimately becomes *his* style, *his* individuality expressed through the medium of dance. Thus there is an infinite variety of substyles, but for the sake of taxonomy, we will discuss only three: (1) traditional style; (2) Oklahoma style; and (3) Northern style, because all three have predominated on the Plains.

The Traditional Style

This is the original Grass dance style, which was popular during the mid-nineteenth century and which still survives through performances by some of the older conservatives. It was also the typical "show" dancing of the Buffalo Bill tours. The characteristic features are the concentrated use of the head and shoulders; the full exposure of the face and chest, suggesting a sense of arrogance or pride; and little concern with footwork other than keeping time to the music. The entire upper torso dances; the face is alive with expression, an explicit awareness of enjoying the dance. Traditional-style dancers are similar through all tribes. There is some vestige of traditional style in Oklahoma, but for the most part it survives on reservations. The younger generation looks upon traditional style as old-fashioned, but the older generation looks with admiration at the few exponents of this style and agree that this is *ikcewacipi*, "real dancing," or *ikceLakota*, "old-time *Indian*."

The Oklahoma Style

This style, the one most often reported as *the* "Pan-Indian" style, originated in Oklahoma at the turn of the twentieth century. It was disseminated in urban areas by relocated Indians, eventually reaching all over the nation. The major differences between Oklahoma style and traditional style are the former's faster tempo and emphasis on fancy footwork, with less regard for head and shoulder movements. There are abrupt changes in posture with quick spins and dips. It has become the accepted contest and show dance at intertribal gatherings in Oklahoma and urban areas, and in the mid-1950s was popular at Pine Ridge for possibly five years.

The Northern Style

Like the Oklahoma Fancy War dance, the Northern style seems to have originated at the time of World War I. Its greatest exponents are the Cree, Three Affiliated Tribes, Plains Ojibwa, Canadian Lakota, and Dakota, as well as the Lakota of Standing Rock, Cheyenne River, and recently Rosebud and Pine Ridge (in the order of diffusion). The Northern style took root in Pine Ridge about 1960, although Northern dancers had always participated in the Sun dance secular events to some degree.

It differs from both traditional and Oklahoma style in its footwork and body movements, although it employs more traditional-style elements than does the Oklahoma style. Characteristically, Northern dancers shake their shoulders, sway their torso (from the hips) from side to side, dart suddenly, changing their direction of dance, and employ a series of trick steps giving the appearance that they are off balance, but they always gracefully recover.

What is most significant is the attitude of the younger Northern dancers: "cool," "hip" (many wear dark glasses); they convey a feeling that they are dancing for themselves, within themselves, but spasmodically and furiously, as if suddenly shaken from a deep narcosis. In contrast with the Oklahoma style, the Northern dancer is not committed to the viewing public but only to himself; yet periodically in the song he becomes alive with enthusiasm in his movements.

In 1960, the Oglala were somewhat skeptical, if not derisive, about the "North Dakota" influence. While the North Dakota Lakota simply called their particular style *Peji Waci,* "Grass dance," the Oglala called it *Galala Waci,* "Ribbon dance," because the Northern dancers wore long fringes on their back aprons. The conservative Oglala described the most significant part of the dance as *iglucancan,* a verb meaning "to shake oneself," and explained that the dancers wore "raggy" costumes (instead of using chainette fringe, some dancers cut fringe from cotton cloth). Today, conservative Oglala prefer that which is "traditional" to that which is "North Dakota," but the Northern style, it would appear, has found some acceptance at Pine Ridge.

War Dance Songs

It is unquestionably in the music that the Pan-Teton group makes its greatest contribution to Pan-Indianism. Music composed at Pine Ridge is finding its way into the repertory of singers outside the Pan-Teton complex. First, this is possible because War dance music of all Plains tribes is interchangeable. Second, Oglala music is particularly vital; new pieces are composed every year. The Oglala today also draw heavily from the north and have become prime instruments in diffusing Northern music to Oklahoma as well as to urban areas.

The War dance song is generically described by the Oglala as *Omaha olowan,* "Omaha song." Certain songs have words, while others have only vocables (Powers 1961a). This is one of the major links in the Pan-Teton structure: that every word-song is mutually intelligible by the seven tribes. Consequently, word-songs diffuse rapidly within the Pan-Teton structure.

But, just as there are primary dance styles, there are also related song styles, and at Pine Ridge traditional songs, although still vital at tribal events, are frequently replaced by Northern-style songs, that is, songs diffusing from "North Dakota," at larger celebrations such as the Sun dance.[4] However, the Oglala have never included Oklahoma songs in their War dance repertories.

Traditional Songs

The majority of Omaha songs of this category have words, and many can be traced to pre-reservation days. Densmore (1918) recorded similar songs among the Hunkpapa at Standing Rock. The peculiarities of the traditional songs, however, are more closely related by their structure and the style in which they are sung. All traditional songs begin with a particular kind of introductory phrase containing vocal ornamentation—sometimes resembling animal cries. They are sung three or four times through and end with a brief coda called *sinte*, "tail." The music is accompanied by drumming—a steady, pulsating beat periodically emphasized with accented duple beats. Some traditional songs end without drum accompaniment. Like other song styles typical of the Plains, the melodic lines are constructed on a descending or cascading scale.

Oklahoma Songs

Songs composed in Oklahoma have not diffused to the Oglala, although the reverse is true. Basically, the Oklahoma song style is closely related to the Oglala traditional style, but the songs are sung in a lower register. Oklahoma Indians agree that the Lakota sing "really high." When Oglala songs diffuse to Oklahoma, their register is lowered and phonetics are altered to conform to Oklahoma vocables.

Northern Songs

All three styles conform to a basic song structure; however, Northern songs have several characteristics which make them unique. They are, first of all, sung in a much higher register than either of the two previous styles. Many traditional singers are unable to employ this vocal technique. The introductory phrase of the songs is sung soprano (some Oglala refer to these voices as "tenors") in elongated, sustained, clear tones. The coda is repeated, often more times than the theme proper of the song. Often the drumming decreases in volume at the end of the song until it is inaudible; the last beat is accented. Many of the "new powwow" songs on the Teton reservations are Northern, not traditional. Their origin may be traced to the Canadian Plains.

Procession

At one time there were no processions as such in Pine Ridge. The Oglala did perform a "Snake" dance in the 1960s which usually took place at least once during each day of the celebration, in order to count the dancers. The length of the dance depended on how quickly the committee tallied the dancers. The step was the common War dance step; the movement, follow-the-leader in a counterclockwise direction. This was obviously a copy of the Snake and Buffalo dance of Oklahoma, and any Omaha song could be used as accompaniment. In the 1970s, the Snake dance was replaced by the Grand Entry, which resembles the Oklahoma procession.

The Round Dance

This has never been as popular a dance at Pine Ridge as in Oklahoma. The Lakota have several circle dances, most of which are related to former war societies and to the women's Victory dance, in which female relatives of warriors carried trophies of war. The Round dance is most conspicuous at other Pan-Indian functions, especially in Oklahoma. At Pine Ridge the Round dance is called *Naslohan Wacipi*, "Dragging Feet dance," so called because of its particular sidestepping movement. It was commonly referred to in the late 1940s and early 1950s as the *Kangi Wacipi*, "Crow dance," which was originally a dance of the *Kangi yuha okolakiciye*, "Crow Owners Society," and appropriate Crow Owner songs were used for its accompaniment. Another circle dance, *Tokala Wacipi*, "Fox dance," a remnant of the *Tokala Okolakiciye*, "Fox" or "Kit Fox Society," was also popular during the late 1940s and early 1950s. Both societies have been described by Wissler (1912).

Round Dance Songs

While there is a class of songs specifically sung for *Naslohan Wacipi*, some with patriotic themes, others with vocables or English lyrics, they are not as popular as Omaha songs. Between the Oklahoma and Oglala songs, tribes outside the Pan-Teton complex consider Oklahoma Round dance songs more melodic ("prettier").

The Forty-nine

The Forty-nine has never received a strong reception at Pine Ridge, although there was some attempt to perform the dance in the late 1930s or early 1940s. The Oglala performed it indoors, dancing in mixed couples under blankets. It was allegedly suppressed by the government superintendent because of licentiousness.

Forty-nine Songs

Forty-nine songs composed on the Teton reservations resemble Oklahoma songs rhythmically but are unrelated melodically. The Tetons prefer word-songs sung partially in Lakota and partially in English.

Stomp Dance

The Creek-Seminole style of Stomp has never reached the Oglala. There is, however, a dance called *Nasto Wacipi*, which translated means "Stomp dance," in which the dancers prance to the accompaniment of a slow, steady beat of the drum, which changes to a fast Omaha dance. There are many Stomp dance songs identical in structure. The Stomp dance as performed at Pine Ridge and Rosebud is part of the "North Dakota" influence, and is also popular at Cheyenne River and Standing Rock. It reached the Oglala in the early 1960s, and continues to be popular as a contest song.

Contests

While the Oklahoma groups seem to thrive on contests, there are relatively few in Pine Ridge. In fact, the idea of a contest reached Pine Ridge only in the early 1960s. Up to that time, one heard many dancers brag of their "championships," but these were usually won off reservation. There once were War dance contests at most of the smaller powwows, and at the annual Sun dance, but interest is on the decline. The contests are officiated (as the Oglala say) "Oklahoma style." The Oglala admit that stopping on the last beat of the drum was never considered important until they heard of it in Oklahoma. The typical characteristic of the Oglala contest is endurance. The War dance songs, in contrast with the twice-through version in Oklahoma, may be sung through eight or nine times. The dancers must keep in time, and loss of an article of costuming means immediate disqualification. Most War dance champions at Pine Ridge and Rosebud are in their late teens. Most contests take place at urban powwows or at reservation fairs.

Powwow Princess

Like the contest, the selection of the powwow princess is new; it became popular in the early 1960s. At the 1966 Sun dance, there was for the first time a powwow princess selected from candidates from each of the reservation districts—similar to the Oklahoma method of selecting from candidates of representative Oklahoma tribes. The powwow princess at Pine Ridge, however, never played a particularly important role at the Sun dance, whereas the Oklahoma princess, with the head dancer, leads the Round dance and Two-step.

Head Dancer

There are no head dancer roles at Pine Ridge.

Tail Dancer

There are no tail dancer roles at Pine Ridge, although they were common up through the 1940s.

Whip Dancer

Whip dancers were common through the late 1940s, but have not been witnessed since. These dancers were originally members of the *Omaha Okolakiciye*, "Omaha Society," described by Wissler (1912).

Whistle Bearers

According to Howard,[5] certain dancers may prolong the dance by blowing their whistles over the heads of the singers. This is a Northern influence popular at Pine Ridge in the early 1960s.

Female War Dancers

These have never been popular at Pine Ridge; however, in 1965 at least one War dance contest in Rapid City, South Dakota, was won by a young lady dressed as a male. It might be well to note that Oglala singers were impressed by a group of female War dance singers from Crow Agency, Montana, who performed at many of the North Dakota powwows.[6]

Giveaway

Otuȟ'anpi, "giveaway," has always been a popular custom at Pine Ridge, and still survives at smaller powwows and other functions of a religious or secular nature. In the giveaway ceremony, one gives something of value or money to another, usually in honor of a deceased relative. At Pine Ridge there are appropriate giveaway songs in which the singers mention the name of the deceased. All transactions are handled through the *eyapha,* "announcer," who states the intentions of the donor. The singers are also recipients of donations. Giveaway was always popular at all events, but has decreased at the Sun dance powwows because it interrupts dancing time.[7]

Feast

The *wohanpi,* "feast," takes place at all Oglala functions. Buffalo meat is normally served at the Sun dance; beef, at smaller functions. Dog meat is still served to the older men and women.[8]

Committee

The committee, called *mazaša yuha,* "has the penny (money)," is the sponsor of the powwow. The Oglala Sioux Tribal Council elects a committee to organize the Sun dance, but all smaller functions are run by committees chosen from within the district in which the powwow takes place. The committee has always been an Oglala institution, dating back to war and chief societies.

Flag Songs

Since World War II the Oglala have had a Flag song which they call the "National Anthem," and which serves that purpose at most tribal events. During the raising and lowering of the American flag, it is sung by an individual over a public address system, or by a group with drum accompaniment. The words are:

Tunkašilayapi tawapaha kin oihankešni he najin kte lo. Iyoĥlate kin oyate kin cana wicicagin kta ca lecamon welo.

The flag of the United States will stand forever.
Beneath it the people will live on.
That is why I do this [honor the flag].

The Flag song is sung on all Lakota reservations; however, each reservation has its own set of words which are similar but not identical. During the Flag song, the people rise and men remove their hats.

Specials

As in Oklahoma, there are a number of specialty dances. Most are specifically Pan-Teton in nature and have not been diffused to other reservations or urban areas. The dances most often performed are the following:

1. The *Maštincala Wacipi,* "Rabbit dance" (Powers 1962a), which is choreographically similar to the Oklahoma Two-step. There is a class of Rabbit dance songs which are used exclusively as accompaniment. A dance similar to the Rabbit dance is called Owl dance in North Dakota.

2. The *Tunweya Wacipi,* "Sneak-up" (literally, "Scout dance"), is probably related to a warrior society. It is danced by a line of men who simulate the actions of warriors. There is only one Sneak-up dance song (Powers 1962b).

3. The Kettle dance, *Ceĥohomni Wacipi,* "They dance around the kettle" dance, sometimes called "Pot dance," is a custom originally observed in the Grass dance. It is danced prior to the feast. The dancers, two or four of whom are armed with forked sticks, pass around the kettle, finally spearing prime pieces of dog meat contained within. This dance has been routinized since the late 1950s for use as a show dance at the Intertribal Ceremonial at Gallup, New Mexico, as well as at other public performances. There are five separate Kettle dance songs, which are sung in specific order.

4. The Hoop dance, *Cangleška Wacipi*, "Hoop Dance," is rarely seen as a show dance, although it was popular as a show dance during the 1940s and 1950s.

5. Miscellaneous. There are a number of dances related to former societies which are occasionally performed in conjunction with smaller powwows. Honor songs are frequently sung to recognize important individuals.[9]

Men's Costumes

The traditional Lakota costume circa 1900 consisted of a porcupine and deer tail headdress, beaded or porcupine quilled moccasins, cuffs and armbands, bone chokers and breastplates, and beaded and sequined aprons. The basic body attire was either dyed long underwear or shirts and trousers of non-Indian manufacture. The "bustles" were clusters of predatory bird and gallinaceous fowl feathers arranged rather haphazardly, thus leading some observers to call them "mess bustles." The earlier "crow belt" was also popular. There was no particular attempt to match the beadwork and featherwork. Many old-timers wore traditional "chief suits," consisting of a warbonnet, and matching buckskin shirts and leggings.

In the late 1940s and early 1950s there was a gradual decline in traditional costumes; in the mid-1950s the typical dance costume was replaced by a poorly simulated Oklahoma Fancy dance costume. For about five years there seemed to be no direction to Oglala costume styles; outlandish substitutes for costumes were used. Then in the 1960s the North Dakota fringed costume began to appear. Although the Northern costume featured the common hair roach, decorated "choke springs" were inserted in place of eagle feathers. There was a marked absence of "bustles." The outstanding characteristic of the costume was the heavily fringed back apron, and matching shirts and pants (usually black) which had V-shaped designs outlined in long ribbon and chainette fringe. The costume was replete with heavy matching beadwork: the gallus was much longer than that worn in Oklahoma, sometimes reaching to the ankles. Belts were wider; cuffs, larger. Many dancers wore sneakers instead of moccasins. Accessories for this costume were not limited to beadwork. Sequins, rhinestones, and miscellaneous items from the local dry goods stores were used as decorations. Individual ornamentation was highly creative, yet all the costumes were definitely discernible as "northern."

Since the 1970s, the Oglala and Sicangu at Rosebud have somewhat modified the North Dakota costume into what they call the "real Sioux" or "New Sioux" outfit. It is necessarily a combination of the Oklahoma and North Dakota styles, retaining the tailored bustles of the South and the fringe and heavy beadwork of the North.

Since the end of the 1970s, old-time costumes have become popular again. While many of the older conservatives have costumes from the 1900 period, few of them wear them at powwows.

Women's Costumes

While many of the women still own traditional dresses with characteristic full beaded yokes, most of them wear homemade cotton dresses or dresses of non-Indian manufacture. All, however, wear hand-fringed shawls, or substitutes, when they dance. This has led the announcer to refer to the women as "shawl dancers."

Peyote Paraphernalia

For all practical purposes Peyote paraphernalia does not exist as a dancer's costume accessory.

Patriotic Organizations

As in Oklahoma, various Indian patriotic organizations are active at powwows.

OKLAHOMA ELEMENTS FOUND IN PAN-TETONISM

By comparing elements found in Oklahoma Pan-Indianism with those in Pan-Tetonism, it becomes clear which Oklahoma or non-Indian elements have infiltrated the Pan-Teton complex. The most outstanding (in the order of their frequency) are (1) the Fancy War dance style, with its related costume; (2) the contest, which is beginning to decline except at urban powwows and fairs; (3) the powwow princess; (4) the procession, which now is represented at Pine Ridge by the Grand Entry; and (5) female war dancers.

Compared with the total number of elements comprising Pan-Tetonism,[10] the above elements represent about 20 percent of the

Pan-Teton aggregate. Round dance, Forty-nine, Stomp dance, the Oklahoma "specials" (with the exception of the Hoop dance), the head and tail dancers, and the appearance of Peyote paraphernalia do not exist at all in Pan-Tetonism. This accounts for approximately 50 percent of Oklahoma elements which *do not* manifest themselves in Pan-Tetonism. The remaining 30 percent represents common Plains elements that are present in both Oklahoma Pan-Indianism and Pan-Tetonism.

On the other hand, of the 20 percent of Oklahoma elements found in Pan-Tetonism, half have been influenced by the North Dakota style (War dance, contest, and whistle bearer), so that essentially very little of Oklahoma Pan-Indianism exists in Pan-Tetonism.

PAN-TETON ELEMENTS FOUND IN OKLAHOMA PAN-INDIANISM

The Pan-Teton complex also contributes certain elements to the Pan-Indian aggregate. The most important is music, but Teton music is not supplanting Oklahoma music; it merely influences it. It appears that more and more Teton, or at least "Northern," songs will influence Pan-Indian singers off the Lakota reservations.

The only other elements influencing the Pan-Indian aggregate are (1) the Northern style of War dance and (2) men's costuming. These influences are being strongly felt in urban areas. Only a few Northern dancers have appeared in Oklahoma, and at this time the Oklahomans are skeptical of their intrusion. It is difficult to predict how popular Northern style will be in Oklahoma—if it ever is—but its influence is certainly a major factor among the Oglala, and it would appear that by accepting the Northern complex, which is basically Pan-Teton, the Oglala are essentially striving to adhere to that which is Lakota rather than that which is "Indian."

OGLALA: SURVIVAL VERSUS REVIVAL

The connotation of Pan-Indianism is not only nationalization but also survival. But in what direction is Pan-Indianism leading the American Indian? Will he ever reach the point where tribal identity is lost in a potpourri of "Indianness"? Will Oglala tribalism be submerged in a Pan-Teton complex, to be lost later in a true Pan-Indian aggregate? I think not. Rather, might not Pan-Indianism lead its members into a stronger appreciation of tribalism? Let us briefly examine recent Oglala history, as well as some significant movements in Oklahoma.

Authorities do not agree in which direction Pan-Indianism is leading American Indians. While there is a definite trend toward similarity of religious, economic, and political thought, the trends of dance and dance costumes are less predictable. A priori one should assume that there is a trend toward the disintegration of tribalism. However, even in Oklahoma, which is considered the cradle of Pan-Indianism, several tribal functions have been revived in the prime of the Pan-Indian movement. Among these are the Ponca rejuvenation of the Hethuska, the Kiowa Black Legging Society, and the Kiowa-Apache Black Foot Society. While these survivals may not be based entirely on distinctively tribal functions of the nineteenth century, they nevertheless are an indication that active tribes need something more than the homogeneity of Pan-Indianism to fulfill their identity as Indians (Powers 1966b).

The Oglala had at least one significant revival in 1959, when the Sun dance, including its self-torture, was performed. Before that time the U.S. government had prohibited the torture. Since 1959 the Sun dance has been performed every summer, each year with more and more dancers participating in the "piercing."

There are some other revivals of lesser importance. The Kettle dance has been performed occasionally on the reservation; earlier it survived only as a show dance performed off the reservation. A change in the character of the dance has occurred: there is today more religious symbolism involved than was true when I first witnessed the "traditional" form in 1949. In general, an attitude prevails today that whatever is "old-time" is similarly "religious." Because of this attitude, revived secular events may assume a new, religious significance.

Some women, at least at the smaller functions, are dancing "old-time," that is, simply bobbing in place around the outer perimeter of the dance area. This was the old Oglala style of dance until the mid-1950s, when, under the Oklahoma influence, women began to dance in the same area as the men. Another change is that, at the larger functions, the Oglala women dance clockwise around the men, performing the "walking" step of the Oklahoma women.

However, they dance on the inside of the circle near the center pole, in contrast with the Oklahoma women, who dance among the men and in the same direction.

Further, women do not wear traditional costuming to the extent they did before the mid-1950s; they simply wear shawls over cotton dresses. They still own traditional costumes but, like the men, now consider them "antiques" and hesitate to risk damaging them by use. A great deal of men's costuming reminiscent of the 1940s and early 1950s has been worn since the 1966 Sun dance celebration. Such costuming was not prevalent in the late 1950s and early 1960s, and indicates a strong preference for tribalism.

While there are bilingual announcements at the larger celebrations, at the small functions they are in Lakota. Many public signs are written in Lakota, and Lakota books are still published at the local schools.

Another subject reported elsewhere (Powers 1977, 1982, 1986) is the retention of religious practices. *Yuwipi,* the sweat lodge, and vision quest are still popular rituals even among the younger generation.

It would appear that if the behaviors which are Pan-Indianism do not lead directly to tribalism, they at least give tribal members an opportunity to reconsider the vitalization of important ceremonies and customs.

It also appears that with the strong North Dakota influence of the 1960s, which was characteristically more conservative than Oklahoma Pan-Indianism, what appears as "new" to the Oglala is really a revival. A case in point is the custom of begging from tent to tent by a group of singers. This custom, called in English "Doorway" or "they dance in front of the doorway," was introduced at the 1962 Sun dance as a North Dakota custom. Upon investigation, however, I discovered that it was also observed at Pine Ridge "a long time ago," and is related to what Densmore (1918) calls "Begging dance."

SUMMARY

Pan-Indianism has been treated as an aggregate which has not been sufficiently investigated. It comprises elements, which may be traced to either a tribal or a non-Indian origin, which in turn evolve and change. Within Pan-Indianism there is a smaller but equally vital complex which may be called Pan-Tetonism.

By comparing the elements of Oklahoma Pan-Indianism with Pan-Tetonism we find that fewer Oklahoma traits than North Dakota traits influence the Oglala. Although there was a strengthening of Oklahoma Pan-Indianism in the mid-1950s, the prominent features are being replaced by Northern traits. This gives the impression that the Oglala still maintain a closer allegiance to that which is Lakota than to that which is "Indian."

There is some indication that Pan-Indianism may be directing American Indians to a stronger appreciation of tribal traits. The Oglala, as well as some Oklahoma tribes, have brought about such revivals. There is also some indication that forgotten customs may reappear under the guise of modern innovations.

Chapter 7

Pan-Indianism Reconsidered

In this new era of anthropological self-evaluation, reinvention, and rethinking, Pan-Indianism as a conceptual category stands as a likely candidate for reconsideration. It is the purpose of this chapter to examine and evaluate just what this concept has told us about the nature of cultural dynamics, what it has not told us, and what it still might tell us. From the vantage point of retrospect, I plan to examine Pan-Indianism beginning with the seminal article by Howard (1955) and ending with the same author's article on the diffusion of the Gourd dance (1976), which he regards as an index of Pan-Indianism. This period of evaluation is partly pragmatic and partly ritualistic: from a practical perspective, the concept of Pan-Indianism was never sharply defined before Howard's initial article, and little new has been added to the literature since his 1976 article; from the point of ritual, this evaluation serves as a means of underscoring the value which I place on Howard's contributions, even though I do not always agree with his conclusions. Furthermore, in selecting the period 1955–1976, I do not mean to suggest any finality in the use or usefulness of the concept of Pan-Indianism, nor do I intend to demonstrate that an idea has come full cycle. Rather, I hope to investigate the persistence of a method of thinking about cultural dynamics which is still very much an integral part of American anthropology, one epitomized in the Pan-Indian model.

I approach the subject chronologically and critically evaluate, with little exception, only those contributions to anthropological literature that consciously address themselves to the problem of

Pan-Indianism. Even the most cursory scan of the literature shows that the concept has been so well embedded in the literature that relatively few authors even cite Howard's original article. Hence, Pan-Indianism is regarded, particularly in recent literature, as a generic fait accompli, somewhat analogous to Van Gennep's rites of passage (1960), a concept also customarily employed without proper citation. The generic status imparted to Pan-Indianism alone makes it eligible for critical and retrospective reconsideration.

THEORETICAL ANTECEDENTS

As I shall demonstrate, there is no singularly acceptable definition of Pan-Indianism to date, partly because it is the product of several schools of thought which are often considered opposed to each other. Pan-Indianism is a logical offshoot of cultural evolution, on the one hand, and of Boasian historicism, on the other. The former logically leads to needs to explain culture contact, and particularly acculturation and assimilation. The latter requires that the notion of "tribe" be given some absolute ontological status. Without a well-defined notion of tribe, there would be no basis for "discrete" populations to commingle and share each other's cultural traits. What both schools have in common, however, is a philosophical and epistemological grounding in Euroamerican ideology with a particular predilection for what Harris has called a "snobbish definition of progress" (Harris 1968:292). Hence, a general theory emerges: when cultures come into contact, they may peacefully coexist; they may share traits along a continuum of variation; or one dominant society may subordinate another to the extent that the latter may disintegrate. Disintegration theory is most frequently associated with ideas about Pan-Indianism, for instance, that Pan-Indianism is a final stage before assimilation into a dominant culture (Howard 1955).

It cannot be overemphasized that Pan-Indianism is simply a variation of acculturation and assimilation studies, which have been the preoccupation of American anthropology since the 1920s. But even those anthropologists who examined the phenomenon of acculturation often did so with some skepticism as to the explanatory power of the term. Kroeber, for example, believed that acculturation "has no doubt been operative since there have been separate human cultures" (1948:234). The surge of interest in it surprised him, leading him to wonder:

> If any modification of one culture by another is acculturation, why the sudden interest, almost excitement, beginning about 1920–25 and culminating perhaps in 1935–40, about a concept as wide, elusive, and protean as this. (ibid.)

Kroeber lists a number of reasons for what he considers the vogue of acculturation studies. First, he says, after World War I the world, or part of it, underwent the beginnings of an Americanization process. There was a need in this country to Americanize various immigrant groups. At the same time more field studies were being done by anthropologists, and it was possible to see firsthand sometimes great changes that native peoples were undergoing as a result of their contact with industrial nations. Also, acculturation studies were seen as contemporary, and therefore practical.

With customary insight, Kroeber also claims that acculturation studies relied partly on what the anthropologist knew about his own society as well as about the natives. And "often it was *easier* to describe this patent, obtrusive mixture [of cultures] than to reconstruct the native primitive culture before it went all to pieces" (ibid.:234–35; emphasis added).

It was this "unconscious hold of ethnocentrism" that led anthropologists to prefer studying hybrid and "bastard" derivatives of their own culture rather than to attempt to understand cultures with radically different patterns and assumptions. Acculturation studies were like "catching the dynamics of culture change in the act" (ibid.:235).

It is pretty much out of this milieu that Pan-Indianism arose and, contrary to Kroeber's predictions, lasted far past the 1940s, and in fact still maintains a respectable place in American anthropology.

In 1955, Howard credited Petrullo with alluding to concepts compatible with his own observations (but also see Mead 1932). First, Petrullo believed that the reservation system had resulted in sympathetic relationships between tribes leading to common social intercourse. Second, he believed that the constant interchange of ideas between Indian tribes was producing a novel sense of nationalism. Last, he stated that cultural exchange between tribes was of primary importance in contributing to the disintegration of tribal culture patterns.

Howard also paid homage to Karl Schmitt, who before his untimely death had presented a paper to the Central States Anthropological Association entitled "A Possible Development of a Pan-Indian Culture in Oklahoma" (Howard 1955:215). Howard also cites the work of William Newcomb, Jr., on Delaware acculturation (Newcomb 1955). Thus Howard was the first consciously to use the term "Pan-Indian" in a published work, but it should be emphasized that he was writing about observations among Oklahoma Indians which were based on fieldwork in 1952 and 1954.[1] The diagnostic features for Howard were the same as for Petrullo, particularly the proximity of tribes in Oklahoma, which led to what Howard defined as "the process by which [Native American] sociocultural entities . . . are losing their tribal distinctiveness and in its place are developing a nontribal 'Indian' culture" (ibid.). Also consonant with Petrullo's ideas was the contention by Howard that:

> Pan-Indianism is, in my opinion, one of the final stages of progressive acculturation, just prior to complete assimilation. It may be best explained as a final attempt to preserve aboriginal culture patterns through intertribal unity. How long this pan-Indian culture will continue is dependent on a number of largely unpredictable factors, such as economic conditions, population shifts, and future miscegenation. (ibid.:220)

Here it is important to note that Howard discusses the implications of Pan-Indianism in terms of an opinion, not a theory. There are also two important editorial idiosyncrasies in the above-quoted material which underscore Howard's caution: "pan-Indianism" is not capitalized, and "Indian" is placed in quotes.

Howard's essential focus was on Oklahoma music, dance, and material culture related to both domains. Here he followed the tradition of two earlier authors, Willard Rhodes and John Gamble (though he apparently was not familiar with their work), both of whom contributed articles to Sol Tax's *Acculturation in the Americas* (1967). Rhodes (1967), tracing his theoretical underpinnings to Kroeber, suggested that English words employed in Native American songs served as an index of acculturation, an idea which has not yet been demonstrated.[2] Gamble (1967) discussed changing dance patterns among the Kiowa, comparing old dances with new and demonstrating the effect of the latter on what he called "intertribal" dances. Howard (1955) and Gamble (1967) came to the same conclusions independently that music, dance, and other aspects of the Plains War dance or powwow were "the prime secular focus of pan-Indianism" (Howard 1955:216).

There were other foci, of course—religion (the Native American Church[3] as the prime example) and political (the National Congress of American Indians and similar associations)—but the primary observation up through Howard's 1955 article were drawn from Oklahoma, itself a unique configuration of American Indian tribes and expressive cultures. To say that what was observed in Oklahoma was also true in other culture areas was not the major contention of these writers. However, soon enough, Pan-Indianism was to be reified in such a way that it would attempt to explain the amalgamation of ideas and traits in other cultural domains and other culture areas.

Writing in 1957, Vogt was to define Pan-Indianism as "an emerging state in American Indian acculturation (1957:139; see also Voget 1956:259), one comprising Pan-Plains elements. He emphasized that:

> The significance of this Pan-Indianism in general terms is that it provides a social and cultural framework within which acculturating Indian groups can maintain their sense of identity and integrity as Indians as long as the dominant larger society assigns them to subordinate status (1957:146).

Vogt further states that "This Pan-Indianism is assuring a forum in which increasing numbers of American Indians are participating in customs and institutions that are describable only as *Indian*" (ibid.:145; emphasis added). Again as an editorial note, I call attention to the fact that "Pan-Indianism" is now capitalized, and "Indian" is without quotes. This incautious use of a generalized notion of Indian leads us to ask just what an Indian trait might be. By giving ontological status to the notion of tribe, logically speaking, there is no such trait or series of traits that can be so generalized. But Vogt adds another dimension to his definition of Pan-Indianism—that of

Pan-Plains elements—and by inference suggests that Pan-Indianism can explain the amalgamation of traits other than music, dance, and material culture.

In an influential book by Hagan, the notions of Pan-Indianism are accepted as a fait accompli. He writes:

> When tribal identity became blurred, one of the great objectives of the reformers was accomplished, but the stubborn Indians refused to become white men. Instead, as their unique tribal characteristics withered away, they replaced them with practices borrowed from other Indians. As with the peyote cult which generated the Native American Church, so with the songs, dances, and handicrafts. Intertribal contacts in the boarding schools and the crowding together of tribes into smaller areas led to a considerable culture exchange and standardization. Formerly inveterate enemies visited each other's settlements and contributed to the rise of a Pan-Indian movement. (Hagan 1961:150)

And later:

> The Pan-Indian movement here offers some grounds for belief that assimilation is in sight for thousands. To the extent that participants have given up their distinctive tribal characteristics, the transition to the dominant culture will be eased. After all, Pan-Indianism results from the willingness of the individual to adapt to new practices. (ibid.:170)

There are some remarkable a priori assumptions made in these two paragraphs: tribal identity became blurred, unique characteristics withered away, assimilation in sight for thousands, transition to the dominant culture eased, and the willingness of the individual to adapt to new practices. One may justifiably ask: Are there no alternatives for American Indians? I shall return to this point.

In the same year, by way of emphasis James wrote, "The key to pan-Indianism lies in social relations between Indians and Whites rather than between tribes" (1961:744), which does not substantially differ from the positions of Howard, Vogt, and Hagan. Pan-Indianism, so far, is regarded as a response to the dominant Euroamerican society and culture, one which permits Indian people to retain a certain degree of identity and integrity.

In 1964, the pessimistic, assimilationist views of the preceding authors were attacked by Ablon. Particularly attacking Pan-Indianism as what had been regarded as a degenerative cultural phase, she wrote:

> It would appear from my data that pan-Indian activities in the city have a positive reason for developing and continuing. The pan-Indian movement cannot be written off as a disappearing and faltering last kick, despite the painful appearance of dance costumes often reduced to dyed blue ostrich plumes over leopard skin bikinis, and 49-er songs which were made up the night before. (1964:303)

Ablon concludes that "tribal orientation may be born from the necessity of mingling with members of other tribes," and argues against the use of the term "Pan-Indianism" to refer to "a terminal phase in the assimilation process" (ibid.:304). This is the first major argument against the assimilationist view, one to be followed by a number of distinguished anthropologists. At first reading, Ablon's perspective might have been influenced by her study of urban as opposed to reservation and rural Indian communities, but later we find that her insights are shared by others.

In 1965 a number of publications appeared which focused on Pan-Indianism. Most notable was a special issue of the *Midcontinent American Studies Journal* edited by Stuart Levine and Nancy O. Lurie (1965). Two articles of particular significance to Pan-Indian studies appeared here, one by Lurie and the other by Robert K. Thomas. Lurie's article was an attempt to evaluate the "renascence" in American Indian cultures from the perspective of the Indians themselves. In this article, Lurie makes strong claims that "tribal identity [is] inseparable from Indian identity" (1965:37).

> Many people dislike the anthropologists' term "Pan-Indianism," arguing that pow-wows, the Peyote or "Native American Church," etc., are cases of mutual borrowing and enrichment of different tribes' own cultures. In terms of legal and political action, they recognize a need for tribes to pull together in helping one another to achieve the different tribes' goals and to oppose by concerted action measures threatening to all tribes' distinctiveness. (ibid.)

Lurie also elucidates four major disagreements that native peoples have with the concept of Pan-Indianism:

a. They reject the inference that "assimilated" Indians should be models for emulation.

b. They reject its racist overtones.

c. They reject the recent appearance of pseudo-Indians, some of whom become part of the model.

d. They reject self-aggrandizing individuals who have become subjects of Pan-Indian studies.

These are particularly insightful observations because they initially reflect the values placed on the Pan-Indian model by its subjects and at the same time elucidate some of the weaknesses of the model which I will discuss below. Lurie less successfully attempts a classification of American Indians with respect to their participation in Pan-Indian events:

a. Nationalist (supratribal, generalized Indian)

b. Intertribal (tribal federalist, generalized Indian)

c. Tribal (local community Indian, parochial, reservation)

d. "Country Indian" (grass roots, "real," full bloods).

The problem here is that the typologies suggest a kind of mutual exclusivity that does not exist at the level of reality, although certainly there are American Indians who might fit more neatly along a continuum of any of the above types, if they could be somehow defined more clearly. In particular the "country Indian" type relies on the concept of race to distinguish it from other types, a concept rejected by the very American Indians whom Lurie interviewed. These criticisms, however, are minor, and cannot overshadow the importance of Lurie's major contribution to Pan-Indian studies, particularly her emphasis on the absence of distinction between tribalism and intertribalism.

In the same journal, Robert K. Thomas published an article titled "Pan-Indianism" which was also to have some influence on Pan-Indianism, although in many respects it is closer to the Petrullo-Howard model than Lurie's. Thomas calls Pan-Indianism a "complex social movement . . . the attempt to create a new ethnic group, the American Indian" (Thomas 1965:75). He compares it with the

Ghost dance movement and Native American Church, and stresses that "pan-Plains traits are becoming the new traits of local Indian communities." Thomas believes that Pan-Indianism "has formed a healing bridge between [Indian] factions" (ibid.:81).

All of these ideas are appealing at first reading. However, a more careful scrutiny reveals that to suggest the formation of a new ethnic group is simply contrary to what American Indians are saying. One would also ask just what some of the characteristics of this new ethnic group are, or, even more important, just how Thomas defines ethnicity. I would also point out that if Pan-Indianism, however defined, was a healing bridge, it was not necessarily between Indian factions (certainly it caused as many splits as bridges) but served, and continues to serve, as a bridge between Indian and non-Indian factions. Thomas' emphasis on Pan-Plains traits, harking back to Vogt's evaluation, is, however, instructive, particularly in the music and dance arena. But this is so because Indians may more easily identify or be identified—if indeed we are faced with an identity problem—by non-Indians who have been nurtured on the Plains image.

In my opinion, one of the most important articles in the journal is by Carol Rachlin. It is important because it stresses current Oklahoma Indian events as part of a continuum rather than vestiges of change. Interestingly enough, the article begins with an editorial comment by Stuart Levine:

> The author's conviction perhaps makes the paper which follows
> less a scholarly article than a primary source, a document if you
> will, of the attitudes of a devoted worker in the field. I have chosen
> to include it not in spite of its editorializing, but because of it. . . .
> (1965:84)

Rachlin discusses the contemporary Indian scene in Oklahoma, which she titles "Tight Shoe Night."[4] After distinguishing the major characteristics of tribalism and intertribalism, she makes some insightful "editorial" comments, of which two stand out in my thinking.

> The time has arrived when the administrators of the Bureau of In-
> dian Affairs and anthropologists should stop talking about "The In-
> dian" floating around in time and space. Today we have enough

knowledge to state, administratively and scientifically, what we are talking about temporally, geographically, legally and humanely.

There is no renascence of Indian culture in central and western Oklahoma, because Indian culture there never died in order to be reborn. Missionaries, government personnel, and do-gooders changed and altered Indian life on the surface but not beneath the surface. (Rachlin 1965:99)

This is perhaps the first structuralist criticism of Pan-Indian studies, and it is unfortunate that the article was preceded by what amounts to an apology, for the article, based on empirical evidence from Oklahoma and other parts of Indian America, suggests that Rachlin is perspicacious despite the fact that she strongly attacks some of the fundamental principles of American anthropology, particularly the one-sidedness of acculturation studies and the hollowness of the assimilationist position. I shall return to the criticism of Pan-Indianism below, but here suffice it to say that not all anthropologists were in favor of the major claims of Pan-Indian studies. A momentous trend based on the acculturation/assimilation model was well under way by the mid-1960s and would continue with little opposition.

It should be noted here that among the Pan-Indian literature of 1965 we also find Howard recapitulating his earlier 1955 article in his monograph *The Ponca* (Howard 1965b). The major difference in this later treatment of Pan-Indianism is that he injects more theoretical considerations, mainly stemming from the acculturation studies of Herskovits, who suggests a process akin to Pan-Indianism in his criticism of Mead (Herskovits 1938; Mead 1932). Howard also cites Linton (1943), suggesting that Pan-Indianism may be regarded as part of a larger phenomenon, "nativistic movements" (Howard 1965b:163); he also sees as profitable theoretical considerations of Voget's "reformative nativism" (Voget 1956) and Wallace's "revitalization movements" (Wallace 1956). Howard also expands his ideas about Pan-Indianism by suggesting that although limited to the social (powwow and hand game) and the religious (Native American Church), he sees a potential application of intertribal solidarity to political and economic issues (ibid.:165). Perhaps this is an harbinger of future Pan-Indian studies which will seek to conflate the

Osage Indian girl. *Photographer and date not recorded. Courtesy of Smithsonian Office of Anthropology, Bureau of American Ethnology Collection.*

social, political, economic, and religious spheres, and in doing so will obfuscate the original model, which dealt nearly exclusively with music, dance, and material culture.

In 1966, in discussing the evolution of the Oklahoma feathers costume, I was concerned with the fact that:

> The authorities do not agree in just what direction Pan-Indianism is leading American Indian society. While there is a definite trend toward unity where religious, economic, and political thought is concerned, music, dance, and dance costumes are apparently unpredictable. Logically, one would assume that there is an overwhelming trend toward the disintegration of tribal traits, however, even in Oklahoma, which is considered the cradle of Pan-Indianism, several tribal functions have been revived in the prime of the Pan-Indian movement. (Powers 1966b:6)

Here I would only want to clarify two assumptions. One deals with the logicality of assuming that tribal traits would disintegrate. In retrospect, the assumption has nothing to do with empirical reality but, rather, with the biases and constraints of the acculturation/assimilation model, an American conceit that non-Western cultures must succumb in toto to "dominant" societies. I have elaborated this point in my treatment of Oglala religion (Powers 1977). The second point I would clarify is the term "revival," which I use in conjunction with the Oklahoma tribes' activities. Here I believe I use the word properly, and at the same time I support Rachlin's disinterest in the cognate term "renascence." To call some kinds of trends or movements revivals is appropriate *if* the term is applied to a reestablished tradition which was at an earlier period of time *voluntarily* given up by a society. It is not appropriate, however, to apply the term "revival" to a tradition that recurs if that tradition was forcibly prohibited, in this case by the United States government. Here I would agree with Rachlin that some aspects of American Indian society to which we attribute the term "revival" never in fact desisted; they were "discovered" later by anthropologists who presumed them to be dead. The same perspective on terminology may be applied to concepts such as "nativism" and "revitalization," each of which needs clarification with respect to causal factors.

In an influential popular book, Josephy attributes the rise of Pan-

Indianism to "relocation, education, government programs, social gatherings and political strivings, that bring Indians of different tribes and backgrounds into contact with each other." He also suggests that Pan-Indianism is partly fostered by other "forces of the world," including the ideals of the United Nations, independence of former colonial nations, and the war on poverty and the civil rights movements in the United States, which "have all tended to encourage the emergence of a unifying spirit among the Indians that transcends tribal affiliations or traditions" (Josephy 1968:29).

Of course, with so many attributed causes, any movement could hardly miss. Josephy's misinformed comments are included because they show the extent to which Pan-Indianism has been accepted as a foregone conclusion precisely at the time that tribalism is on the rise.

Although it is now well embedded in the literature, not all authors treat Pan-Indianism with the same sense of absolutism that appeared in the first decade of publishing on it. In 1966 Eggan is still able to give a fresh look at Pan-Indianism when he states:

> Of the 500,000 and more Indians now in the United States, some 60 per cent are still on reservations, and with greater mobility and the development of the Pan Indian movement, the ties between reservation and non-reservation Indians are being *strengthened*. (Eggan 1966:146; emphasis added)

In 1968 Price, in investigating the migration and adaptation of American Indians to Los Angeles, states more cautiously:

> An awakened pan-Indianism . . . often becomes an additional dimension to, and sometimes a substitute for . . . tribal affiliation . . . [and] . . . thus seems to emerge as a stabilizing element—and perhaps a permanent part—of the adaptation of the Indian migrant to the metropolitan areas. . . . (Price 1968:175)

Here I believe that the ideas of Pan-Indianism strengthening tribal ties, on the one hand, and further serving as a stabilizing element, on the other, are important and thus include under the term reservation Indians as well as city migrants.

Perhaps it is the irony of finding tribalism in the city that led anthropologists working in urban areas to become more sensitive to the real motivating factors behind the force called Pan-Indianism. I think that the most insightful work produced by urban anthropologists is that of Hirabayashi, Willard, and Kemnitzer (1972). While in 1971 anthropologists following in the tradition of Howard were still arguing that "Pan-Indianism and the 'return to the Indian way' is not a retrogression but a positive advance toward full integration of Plains Indian groups into the larger American society" (Sanford 1971), urban and applied anthropologists were becoming much more cautious, and therefore productive in understanding Pan-Indianism's capacity to serve as a stabilizing factor between the various tribes and the federal government and others in the white man's world. The irony of the city is that Indians from various reservations and communities who have moved to the cities under government relocation programs are maintaining strict allegiances to their tribes, even to the extent of forming tribal clubs for the purpose of keeping alive what they perceive to be their unique tribal distinctiveness against the overwhelming odds of "assimilation" in the cities.

Hirabayashi et al. distinguish between formal and informal Pan-Indian associations, the former having a structure akin to non-Indian organizations such as social clubs or church groups; the latter, having no formal structure, often are formed from "a common experience with urban institutions such as schools, jobs, relocation offices, bars, and jails" (1972:81).

The authors define Pan-Indianism as "those processes through which Indians of various cultural backgrounds identify and associate with each other." Nationally, they state, many factors "have led to a certain sense of Indian unity, with the BIA as the common adversary" (ibid.:77).

This most refreshing approach goes unheeded, however, since the earlier doomsday predictions, the acculturation/assimilation models, are by now simply taken for granted, particularly by anthropologists, sociologists, historians, and others working with American Indians, many of whom have never had direct contact with the Indian peoples themselves—or, if they did, were so prejudiced by the Pan-Indian model as an *object* of study rather than a *process*, as Hirabayashi and his colleagues have analyzed it, that any indications of a tribal "revival" were overlooked. Of additional importance to Hirabayashi's analysis is that the authors see tribes with fluid social organization tending to join both formal and informal Pan-Indian groups, while those with strong social organization tend not to join many groups. All in all, these authors have given Pan-Indianism a new set of dimensions that work quite well on reservations as well as in urban settings. One can clearly see that on reservations, certain social groups join in more organizations oriented toward dealing with outside forces, such as the BIA and other agencies, while others are content to participate exclusively in the tribal aspects of their distinct culture.

In 1971, two important works on the subject emerged. In one, the presence and persistence of the Howard model is alive and well, although this time with a new twist. In the first complete book devoted to the subject, Hertzberg gives her *The Search for an American Indian Identity* the subtitle *Modern Pan-Indian Movements.*

Hertzberg's study is a history of various individuals and of the organizations which they established, all of them treated under the rubric Pan-Indian. She typologizes national movements into (a) Reform Pan-Indianism: progressive movements at the turn of the century, all of which had the welfare of the American Indian as their objective, with particular emphasis on equality and self-determination; (b) Fraternal Pan-Indianism: mostly dealing with social clubs that became established as increasing numbers of reservation Indians inundated the cities; and (c) Religious Pan-Indianism: which focuses on the Native American Church.

The typologies are not mutually exclusive; for instance, the Ghost dance movement is not "religious" but "reform." Moreover, the leaders of all these forms of Pan-Indianism are regarded by the author as "Pan-Indians," a clear case in which the term has been used so broadly that it could conceivably refer to *all* interrelations between Indian tribes, and between tribes and non-Indians prior to and after contact. Again it is not clear just what traits are being regarded as diagnostic features of Pan-Indianism. For example: "Pan-Indian songs and dances, and tribal adaptations of these" (1971:10) is clearly a nonsequitur, for a tribe does not adapt that which it already owns. In predicting the influence and possible result of Pan-Indian movements, the author states: "Groups will have different degrees of tribal emphasis, they will of necessity assert

George Arkeketah, Oto. *Photo by William Dinwiddie, March 1895. Courtesy of Smithsonian Office of Anthropology, Bureau of American Ethnology Collection.*

a common Pan-Indian bond distinct from or complementary to tribal loyalties" (ibid.:321). Again, this is a statement which covers all possible options for American Indians and therefore is scientifically meaningless.

Hertzberg also regards Pan-Indianism as "subculture" (ibid.:321), but it is not clear what this could possibly mean in the context of her various definitions of it.

Also in 1971, Lurie again broached the subject of Pan-Indianism from a historical perspective that may well stand as one of the most realistic syntheses of contemporary American Indian cultures. Of particular interest is her proposition "that the course and form of modern Indian activities may illustrate a distinctive phenomenon in the field of culture contact and culture change" (Lurie 1971:418). She introduces the term "articulatory movement," which designates a type of movement which is devoid of identifiable leadership and seeks pluralism as a basic goal. It is distinguished from other types of movements, such as the Black Power movement, in that its objectives do not require social and cultural acceptance in the total society on par with other ethnic groups, and differs from revitalization movements in that it does not seek internal reforms (ibid.:418). Lurie further emphasizes:

> Indian identity rests on traits of clearly local, tribal origin, such as language or religion; on traits of white origin so markedly reinterpreted in local terms as to be unique to the community and now part of its *own* culture, such as styles of dress, diet, or specialized occupations; and on traits of both kinds that have become widely diffused from tribe to tribe so as to characterize virtually all Indian groups to some degree. The last is usually designated as Pan-Indianism in the anthropological literature. (ibid.:419; emphasis added).

Lurie sees an articulatory movement as reaching a large public in order to win support for Indian goals leading to a general Indian identity. However, she also sees the possibility that intertribal activities and even the urban situation are part of a complex whole making up articulatory adaptations. She states:

> Thus it is also possible to argue that left to their own devices, tribal communities could persist indefinitely as distinctive and dynamic combinations of local tradition, Pan-Indian elements, and different selections from the larger society. Fundamentally, the present Indian movement is directed toward developing their own devices along these lines in the face of serious opposition. (ibid.:420)

Recognizing that Pan-Indianism "unites Indian people ideologically . . . to provide structures for action" (ibid.:443), Lurie defines Pan-Indianism as "a persisting cluster of core values [and] predictable behavior . . . [Indians] . . . do not share with people of European cultural tradition," which include the following:

a. A preference for reaching decisions by consensus
b. A high value placed on oratory
c. Special Indian humor
d. Patterns of institutionalized sharing
e. Lack of emotional commitment to personal possessions
f. Indirect control of the behavior of others
g. A generalized respect for people
h. Withdrawal from anxiety-producing situations
i. A propensity for being more observant than whites
j. Adaptability to new contact situations.

In speaking of the secular aspects originally treated by Howard, Lurie states that there are two kinds of powwows, "both diffusing Pan-Indian traits and reinforcing tribal identity" (ibid.:540), the latter type being "primarily a community effort in which local customs and language are evident despite the overlay of Pan-Plains elements" (ibid.:451). Finally, citing Ablon, she emphasizes that "Tribal identity even seems to be encouraged by participation in Pan-Indian urban life" (ibid.:469).

Thus Lurie complements Hirabayashi et al. and Price, as well as my own work, in seeing the two-dimensional aspect of the concept of Pan-Indianism as a process. But of course Pan-Indianism is very much like the concepts which it extends—acculturation and assimilation. Thus, anthropologists continue to write about its cause as one related to a conscious amalgamation of traits at the expense of a decrease in tribalism, clearly a set of ideas that cannot be validated empirically. It is as if anthropology has itself formed a bifurcation in which one theoretical lineage continues to promulgate the Howard model, while another attempts to explain the concept quite differently, if not revolutionarily. In Wax and Buchanan (1975), for example, two chapters are titled "Pan-Indian Militancy" (chapter 6), which mainly cites the writings of Vine Deloria, Jr., and "Religious Pan-Indianism" (chapter 7), mainly about the works of Weston LaBarre and Peter Nabokov on the Native American Church.

Again, Pan-Indianism is simply accepted at face value as a meaningful term, which for the editors has been going on since colonial times throughout "a series of movements among the various tribes toward establishing a common identity as Indians" (Wax and Buchanan 1975:162). But certainly, if Pan-Indianism is to be specific, it cannot be seen as an ongoing movement traced back to European contact. Even Howard would not find this idea acceptable. Wax and Buchanan also refer to political, religious, and fraternal forms of Pan-Indianism, obviously in keeping with Hertzberg's earlier idea but without referring to her work specifically.

This leads us finally to Howard's article on the Gourd dance as a revitalization movement (Howard 1976), in which he approaches the subject of Pan-Indianism from a much more tempered point of view, even citing Lurie's 1971 article to partly confirm for himself that Pan-Indianism, however defined, is not so much a doomsday machine as it is a means of establishing that

> Native American culture is far from dead . . . and now and then some aspect of culture long considered lost and forgotten rises phoenix-like from its own ashes to confound those who see only a steady attrition of American Indian culture in the modern world. (1976:243)

Clearly Howard has become a revisionist to his earlier way of thinking about Pan-Indianism and eventual assimilation. In his typical style, that of a seasoned ethnographer, Howard points out that the Gourd dance, once associated with Oklahoma tribes, has become widespread on the Northern Plains as well. As such the Gourd dance is another example of a Pan-Indian movement that he presented to the anthropological world 21 years earlier. But what makes this article different from most of Howard's earlier works is his desire to explain why this particular revival has become prominent, if not successful, as a marker of ethnic identity while others have not. Because the ultimate answer, he believes, would require intensive interviewing of tribal members whose ancestors had performed the Gourd dance, Howard opts for another tactic, that of providing a post hoc rationalization for the popularity of the dance rather than any attempt to discern its causes.

In doing so, Howard opts to employ Anthony F. C. Wallace's now famous processual model of a revitalization movement (Wallace 1956), explaining that the Gourd dance, in the process of diffusion throughout the Northern Plains as well as the Southern Plains, helps young Indians to enjoy a more satisfying culture. Whether or not Wallace's model can account for the Gourd dance data is another type of problem to be addressed. Nevertheless, Howard ends his descriptive article by saying:

"We are all Indians," the Pan-Indian rallying cry, is the common argument used to persuade spectators to become participants. It now seems that the Gourd dance will continue to spread in Native America and increasingly serve as a vehicle for Pan-Indian identification in the modern world. (ibid.:257)

At this stage in the development of ideas on the concept of Pan-Indianism, we might have prematurely discovered that the person who had contributed more than anyone else in the field on the subject had finally come around, as it were, and joined that weakened branch of the bifurcated discipline that really saw Pan-Indianism as a process that stabilized or even fostered tribalism where it never had occurred, such as in urban areas. Theoretically as well as ritually and pragmatically, we might have come full circle to witness a declaration that perhaps Howard had erred in placing perhaps too much emphasis on the assimilative nature of Pan-Indianism, an idea that he had undoubtedly inherited from his teacher, Leslie White. And judging by the pronouncements about the Gourd dance as a revitalization movement, even if the data are mounted on the model rather imaginatively, at least we are not bound to anticipate the end of Indian culture somewhere on the other side of a Pan-Indian powwow of the near future. But such is not the case, as the following example from a 1983 article attests, one written before Howard's untimely death.

As a result of a session organized by myself as a state-of-the-art symposium on American Indian music and dance over the past hundred years, Howard accepted my invitation to present his most recent thinking on the subject of Pan-Indianism. The proceedings of the symposium were never published but some of the individual papers were, including his presentation, "Pan-Indianism in Native American Music and Dance." In this very brief recapitulation, mainly of his own work, Howard was quick to point out that many people saw nothing particularly special about Pan-Indianism, and that what he had originally discussed in his 1955 article was simply part of a larger process of diffusion which included the Ghost dance, Hand game, Sun dance, and other tribal performances usually associated with the Plains and Prairies. Howard was quite adamant in this last paper on Pan-Indianism that this was not the case. He insisted that in the old days new ideas, be they dances or ceremonies, were exchanged between tribes formally, whereas in Pan-Indianism, as he defined the amalgamation of traits, the exchange was informal, perhaps even unconscious. Pan-Indianism for him was simply what young Indians were doing nowadays. After a brief survey of the characteristic forms of Pan-Indianism in various culture areas, Howard ended his piece with a rather strong sentimental statement which enunciated his attitudes about Pan-Indianism over the past three decades.

His concluding statement is worth presenting in its entirety:

> Participation in Pan-Indianism events undoubtedly drains performers or potential performers from more distinct tribal or regional music and dance forms. Younger Indians, like young people everywhere, want to be a part of whatever everyone else is doing, not lonely advocates of tribally specific music and dance styles associated with and known only to a few of their elders. This, in fact, is almost certainly the principal appeal of Pan-Indianism—solidarity with other Indians in a rapidly shrinking Indian world.
>
> Though one may lament the growth of Pan-Indianism in sounding the death knell for many ancient and beautiful Native American songs and dances, such is the way of the world. In most cases these dances and songs would wither and disappear in any case, probably to be replaced by non-Indian music and dance. I will therefore close my essay with what will undoubtedly come to be known as Howard's famous epigram: "Better pan-Indianism than no Indianism." (1983:81)

SUMMARY AND CONCLUSIONS

Historically Pan-Indianism is a logical offshoot of acculturation studies, the difference lying in the cultural and regional specificity of Pan-Indian studies. As such, approaches to Pan-Indian studies have mirrored the same approaches to acculturation studies and fall into three major subtypes: (a) assimilationist, those which predict the total subsumption of American Indian groups by the dominant American society; (b) synthetic, which views the conflation of traits and values of the dominant and subordinate societies as forming a new sense of identity and allegiances; and (c) preservational, which maintains that significant aspects of native society will persist within the context of the dominant society.

Although the assimilationist view has been the most influential, it has been based largely on an a priori assumption about the nature of culture contact: that subordinate societies are somehow predestined to succumb biologically, linguistically, and culturally to the dominant society. However, there has been no empirical evidence that this has happened to American Indian groups. And here it should be reiterated and emphasized that Pan-Indian studies can be concerned only with the dynamic interactions of groups of people, not individuals.

The synthesist view, although interesting theoretically, has not been investigated nationally. It is possible, however, to investigate regional syntheses between American Indian and other national and ethnic groups.

The preservationist approach has been studied little but perhaps provides a more directed future for Pan-Indian studies because empirically we cannot deny that American Indian tribes still exist, and members of these tribes perceive themselves to be different somehow from members of the dominant society, and also perceive themselves to be distinct from other tribes.

Most authors agree that there are aspects of Pan-Indianism that must be treated differentially, the larger types being politics and economics, social institutions, and religion. These have been typed by Hertzberg as fraternal, social, and religious; and by Wax and Buchanan as political, fraternal, and religious. If these types do exist, then I believe it would be rewarding to understand if there are relationships between these types of Pan-Indianism, and if so, just what they are. Even on logical grounds it would seem that by definition Pan-Indianism cannot seriously be regarded as a movement, but perhaps types of Pan-Indianism can be. Rather, Pan-Indianism is more profitably regarded as a complex or a system, perhaps even a higher level of social organization analogous to a segmentary system which unites lower levels of organization (here, American Indian tribes) situationally against the imposition of the dominant society. It appears also that in addition to operational differences, we should examine local and regional differences and similarities in the manner in which Pan-Indian activities manifest themselves.

Although the idea that Pan-Indianism strives towards the creation of a new ethnic group, the American Indian, is novel and interesting, it is unlikely that this definition can be regarded seriously, given what we know about the distinctiveness and variety of American Indian tribal cultures. Furthermore, there is a danger in predicting this kind of synthesis, since the only other means of recognizing a homogeneous population is by turning to the concept of "race" as a diagnostic feature. This would make Pan-Indian studies into a racist doctrine, which, as I have mentioned earlier, is one of its major criticisms by native people themselves. The notion of homogenization also supports the social and political myth that there in fact exists a generalized American Indian. The use of "generalized Indian" as a concept in the Pan-Indian literature simply is undefinable without making reference to tribal contributions to the phenomenon; hence it is a contradiction in terms.

The term "Pan-Indian" as a reference to an individual should be discontinued for the reason stated above. There are tribal members who participate in Pan-Indian events, but this makes as much sense as referring to a New Yorker who participates in the Philadelphia Mummer's Parade as a Philadelphian.

It may be profitable to investigate what has been referred to as reform, or political, Pan-Indianism as a discrete institution analogous to an American political party, one which, like other political parties, exhibits factionalism but is capable of demonstrating unity when confronted by opposing political parties. Like a political party, or perhaps a political system representing many political parties, it recruits its leadership from diverse tribal backgrounds, but its constituents are the individual tribes themselves, and subsequently individual communities and individuals of those constituent tribes.

The possibility of the Native American Church as a religious form of Pan-Indianism should be seriously reconsidered. It is in fact a religious denomination with many regional and local variations, but it cannot be said that it represents any particular trend in a national American Indian religion. With the exception of some tribes in Oklahoma, Peyotism has not made great inroads into the native religious systems of most tribes, and no one has seriously studied whether or not members of the Native American Church leave it to participate in tribal religious activities. In the past the Native American Church has been regarded as if it is analogous to a singular Christian denomination. But empirically the NAC is divided conceptually into two "denominations" and, as Rachlin has shown, enough local variations exist to suggest even finer distinctions.

In the social arena—that aspect of Pan-Indianism which has drawn most of the attention of investigators, and in fact has served as a model for general considerations of Pan-Indianism—we should distinguish between tribalism, on the one hand, and intertribalism, on the other; the two stand in a dialectical relationship to each other. Tribalism symbolizes and operationalizes conservatism and cultural continuity. Intertribalism symbolizes and operationalizes liberality and change, particularly rapid change. Individuals move back and forth between tribal and intertribal ideologies and activities situationally; and they are capable of distinguishing between the two systems. Furthermore, the tribal and intertribal dyadic structure stands in a dialectical relationship between American Indian and non-Indian society. Some elements of non-Indian society move into American Indian society through intertribal events and activities, such as the format of the contemporary powwow, much of which is borrowed from rodeoing. Much of what is tribal also reaches the non-Indian society—politicians, artists, professional people—by means of the intertribal mediation.

Terms such as "revivalism," "nativism," or more broadly "revitalization," with respect to their application to Pan-Indianism, should be used with caution, particularly if customs which are being reestablished were forcibly restricted or prohibited by the federal government as part of its "civilizing" programs. Similarly, the term "identity" should be used sparingly. It is unlikely that all peoples of the world are suffering from an identity crisis with the same kind of uniformity that is suggested in the term. There are enough examples of Americans living abroad participating in a full life without the fear of losing their Americanness. If identity loss, or the blurring of tribalism, is supposed to be real for American Indians, then it should be just as real for others, including ourselves.

Although my own position of favoring the preservationist perspective is perhaps clear and obvious, I believe that there is a future for Pan-Indian studies as long as we do not assume an unwavering assimilationist perspective. We do not know, for example, to what extent the diffusive nature of intertribal enterprises affects the tribalism of a single tribe, much less the whole nation of tribes. Interestingly, the argument becomes increasingly circuitous, perhaps not because this is the nature of scientific inquiry so much as because circuity is the nature of cultural evolution.[5]

Although my point of departure for Pan-Indian studies was acculturation studies, we may trace its origin to even earlier studies. Acculturation is partly born out of the emphasis placed on diffusion by Franz Boas and his students. Their study of how traits diffused logically led to an assumed historical particularism on the part of Boas and his use of the term "cultures," with the emphasis on plurality. If we look at the sequence of scientific inquiries starting with Boas (and of course his teachers, who were essentially human geographers), we find that diffusionism gives rise to particularism, therefore emphasizing the notion of tribe.[6] Enter the European, and we must now explain diffusionism in other terms, that is, acculturation. The general theory of acculturation in its specific form becomes Pan-Indianism, which logically seeks to examine again the diffusion of traits between tribes. This diffusion again logically assumes a notion of particularism, and we are right back where we started in our paradigmatic series.

One final consideration: If Pan-Indianism is to be a viable approach to understanding cultural dynamics, we should probably eliminate the "ism" and regard "Pan-Indian" as a processual model or method of viewing interaction between Indians and non-Indians. As such, the concept of Pan-Indian[7] would serve to complement other kinds of approaches without the need to manufacture a phenomenon which may not be all that important to American Indian peoples themselves.

PART II
Plains Music in Review

Chapter 8

Songs of the Red Man

In David P. McAllester's review of Navajo music (1968:470–471), he alludes to the Canyon Record cover blurb which states that the songs he reviewed were "some of the most representative and requested Navajo songs." McAllester justifiably remarks, "It would be a valuable thing to know who chose what as 'representative,' and which [songs] are the 'most requested.'" He concludes, "An index of what is most popular . . . would tell us a good deal about current directions in American Indian Music."

Linn D. Pauahty, director of the American Indian Soundchief Library, eight albums of which are reviewed here, claims on each cover: "Our library has been recognized by the Indian Tribes of the United States and Canada as the world's foremost authority of songs, music and chants of the Southern and Northern Plains Tribes." Pauahty adds, "Music and songs [are] arranged and sung by various outstanding singers of the Southern and Northern Plains Tribes."

In my opinion, Pauahty's claim is valid. His total library (*Songs of the Red Man*), consisting of songs from over twenty Northern and Southern Plains tribes, provides an accurate index of current Plains Indian musical trends as well as a substantial archive of older, traditional music. There are a number of reasons why Soundchief provides an accurate index. Pauahty is Kiowa and grew up on the Southern Plains. He also has traveled and lived among the Northern Plains Indians since the 1960s and has developed a great appreciation for music of the entire Great Plains area. As in the case of

Canyon and Indian House Records, American Indians are the primary market for Soundchief recordings; thus, to the great disadvan-
tage of the ethnomusicologist, Pauahty does not write extensive
cover liners or independent notes, presumably because Indians do
not require additional information to appreciate their own music.
Finally, Pauahty selects singers from various tribes who are considered exceptional by the tribesmen whom they represent, and the
singers themselves choose the songs they wish to record.

Since most Soundchief albums are arranged categorically by musical "function," there is no question that Pauahty suggests to his
singers specific topics, such as War dance songs or Peyote songs, but
the choice of songs within each category is left to the discretion of
the musicians themselves. In the case of traditional songs, religious
or secular, often the number and order of the songs are predetermined by the nature of the ceremony which the songs accompany.
In the case of the newer, social dance songs, the singers are free to
sing songs which *they* consider best. In the albums reviewed here,
over half the social dance songs have been composed since 1965.
Others are modifications of songs composed prior to 1965. The
majority of Northern War dance songs reviewed here were popular
in 1967–1968. Comparing these with others which I personally
recorded as they were performed by Lakota, Northern Cheyenne,
Arapaho, and Shoshoni singers during this period shows there is no
question that the songs represented here are popular, widely diffused, and very indicative of musical trends on the Northern and
Southern Plains.

Northern Cheyenne War Dance Songs by Tribal Singers, Lame Deer,
    Montana. No. CHYNE-108-B. Sides I and II, six bands each. One
    12″ 33-1/3 rpm disc.
Blackfeet Grass Dance Songs by Allen White Grass, Pat Kennedy, and
    Stanley Whitemen. No. BLACKFEET-100-A and 100-B. Side I,
    five bands; Side II, six bands. One 12″ 33-1/3 rpm disc.
Chippewa-Cree Grass Dance Songs by the Rocky Boy Singers, Paul
    Eagleman, leader. Rocky Boy, Montana. Sides I and II, seven
    bands each. One 12″ 33-1/3 rpm disc.

All songs on these three albums are typical of Northern Plains War
dance songs. The terms "Grass dance" and "War dance" are inter-

Young Arapaho Grass dancer, ca. 1880. Note the neck "bustle," plus beaver breastplate and dew claw bandolier. *Photographer not recorded. Courtesy of Smithsonian Office of Anthropology, Bureau of American Ethnology Collection.*

Omaha dance at Pine Ridge, South Dakota, July 4, 1940. *Photographer unknown. Courtesy of the Heritage Center, Inc.*

changeable. The more conservative tribes use the older form, "Grass dance," while "War dance" is becoming common at intertribal gatherings. There are also other interchangeable tribal terms, such as "Omaha dance" (Lakota) and "Wolf dance" (Shoshoni), but the tribal designations of this popular social dance are being replaced by the English term "War dance." Northern typicality is not evident on two bands of the Cheyenne record: side II, band 5, which may have been borrowed from the Southern Plains; and side II, band 6, which is more rightly a modification of the War dance song called "Stop dance song." This latter song is used often to break ties in War dance contests. The drumming and singing stop abruptly at given points of the song, and unless the dancer, who must stop dancing each time the song stops, knows the song, he is easily eliminated for "overstepping" the beat.

All three albums also have the following in common: all songs are sung with vocables; side I of each album begins with songs in slow or medium tempi, and side II terminates with a series of fast War dance songs usually reserved for contests. With rare exception, each song is rendered three times and ends with the typical "tail" (coda). This formula undoubtedly was followed for recording purposes, as the Northern Plains tribes render the songs as many as twenty times during a dance.

The performance of these songs is representative of the incomplete repetition type and may be formulized as AA¹BCBC-BC.

This form may be further interpreted thus:

A—The introductory phrase, sung by the leader
A¹—The introductory phrase, repeated by the "second" or, at
  times, the entire chorus
B—The theme of the song, sung by the entire chorus
C—The cadence, sung by the entire chorus.

The form AA¹BCBC constitutes, by Indian standards, a complete song. The second half of the song (BC) is sung without the introductory phrase and second, hence the incomplete repetition. The tail is comprised of BC only. There is a slight pause between the final cadence of the song and the beginning of the tail. Three renditions and a tail may be further illustrated thus:

1st rend.   AA¹BCBC
2nd rend.   AA¹BCBC
3rd rend.   AA¹BCBC
Coda   BC.

As the illustration indicates, the introductory phrases of second and third renditions (A) are begun by the lead singer while the chorus is still singing the cadence (C), and one may hear an "overlapping" of voices on all typical songs when sung by a group. (A solo singer singing the same songs arbitrarily may eliminate the second [A¹] or "second himself.") Through an editing error, the introductory phrases are eliminated on *Cheyenne*, Side I, band 2, and *Chippewa-Cree*, Side II, band 3. The tail is also eliminated on the latter band.

Certain qualities of drumming are similar on the three albums. The typical pulsating drumming is heard on all songs, the drum slightly preceding the voice. The volume of voice and drum decreases at the repeat of BC, then builds to a crescendo at the end of the repeat. Accented duple beats are heard in the middle of the repeat of B in each rendition. The accents, varying from four to seven beats, are largely determined by one drummer. The average number of accented beats is five in most Northern Plains songs. The rhythmic form of the drum is usually:

♪♪♪♪♪♪♪♪
x   x   x   x   x

Variations often heard are

♪♪♪♪♪♪♪♪
x   x   x   x

or

♪♪♪♪♪♪♪♪♪♪
x   x   x   x   x

The tempo at the beginning of the second rendition is normally increased, but one has the feeling of a slight ritard at the end of each rendition. The tempo increases again as the next rendition begins.

The Cheyenne and Blackfeet use a commercial bass drum on the recordings, but the Chippewa-Cree do not. Commercial bass drums are very popular and in fact are preferred by Northern Plains singers.

Ideally, each singer beats the drum with a drumstick, either a commercially manufactured bass drumstick or, most often, a home-made stick made from a fiberglass rod around which is wrapped a length of sheepskin. The handles are often taped to prevent slipping.

On the Chippewa-Cree album one can hear the tapping of sticks against the rim of the drum, a common drumming style among the North Dakota, Montana, and Canadian Plains tribes. On the Black-feet album dancers' bells are heard. It is difficult to determine whether someone is actually dancing, or simply shaking the bells for effect.

While I have pointed out the similarities of the three albums, some mention must be made of the uniqueness of each. Each tribal group, while adhering to a typical melodic and rhythmic form of the War dance song, presents interesting anomalies in vocal production, vocabalic structure, and, in some instances, drumming technique.

When referring to vocal types, one may classify the major Northern Plains tribes (by voice coloring and vocabalic structure) into the following categories:

Type A   Plains Cree, Plains Chippewa, Hidatsa, Mandan, Gros Ventre, North Dakota Lakota
Type B   Blackfeet
Type C   Crow
Type D   South Dakota Lakota, Northern Cheyenne, Northern Arapahoe.

Type A, which is represented on the Chippewa-Cree albums, strongly influences tribes of the remaining categories and may be observed occasionally on the Northern Cheyenne album, but not on the Blackfeet. While all Northern Plains tribes sing in a high register, Type A usually is sung the highest. The introductory phrases (A) and "seconds" (A^1) are relatively longer than those appearing in other types, and the introductory vocables are extended in clear, falsetto tones. Often there is a slight pause between the introductory phrase and the second, rather than the interruption by the "second" typical of other tribes. The volume of voice is extremely intense, especially in the lead lines. While the vocables of Type A are the same as in the other types, there is recurrence of the vocabalic formula *we ya yo hi ye* which terminates phrase endings in B of most songs.

The drumming style is characteristically different from that of other Northern Plains tribes. The songs usually begin with the singers tapping on the rim of the drum through AA^1; not until midway through B does the leader strike the center of the drum firmly. Often the rim-tapping is performed at the beginning of each rendition; other times it is used only during the first rendition. At the beginning of the tail, the leader strikes the drum firmly *once* before the group begins the final BC portion of the song. Among some Minnesota Chippewa singers, the drum is often struck firmly *twice* before beginning the "tail."

In Type B, exemplified here on the Blackfeet album, the introductory phrases are sung in a high register, but one is aware of the relative softness in volume and a slight quavering of the lead line, typical of the Blackfeet.

In Type C, not represented on any albums reviewed here, and typical of the Crow, we find a lower register combined with a quavering voice in the lead.[1] A fuller, supported voice is found in

Crow songs, with little emphasis on the falsetto quality of Types A and B.

In Type D, represented here by the Cheyenne, there are traces of an older style characterized by vocal ornamentation in the introductory phrases accompanied by shouts or yelps. The Northern Cheyenne, through long association with the Arapahoe and Lakota, normally sing in Type D style, although on this particular album we find the Type A influence on a few songs. The Type A influence is rapidly spreading among the South Dakota reservations, where it is referred to as "North Dakota" singing. The younger singers of tribes which usually sing in the Type D style are all but exclusively adopting the Type A style as *the* current musical trend.

In types B, C, and D, the vocabalic structures are similar; the cadences (including Type A) are identical with the exception of Type D, where there is a strong presence of the consonant "L," influenced by the frequency of "L" in the Western dialect (Lakota) used in most South Dakota songs.[2]

Crow Tribal Sun Dance Songs by Pete Whiteman and Milton Yellow Mule. No. CROW-705. Side I, seven bands.
Northern Cheyenne Sun Dance Songs by Phil Whitemen, head singer, and Tribal Singers, Montana. No. NORTH.CHYNE-700. Side II, seven bands. One 12" 33-1/3 rpm disc.

The Plains Indian Sun dance has for several decades attracted the attention of anthropologists, historians, artists, journalists, and, recently, cinematographers. A bibliography of references to this annual religious convocation would run into hundreds of titles. Briefly, beginning with Catlin's description of the Mandan Sun dance (1967), the ritual has been described for the Sarsi and Cree of Alberta by Goddard (1919a, 1919b); the Assiniboine by Kennedy (1961); the Crow, Shoshoni, Ute, and Hidatsa by Lowie (1915; 1919); the Plains Ojibwa, Plains Cree, and Sisseton by Skinner (1919a, 1919b, 1919c); the Kiowa by Spier (1921b); the Oglala by Walker (1917), Feraca (1963), and Powers (1977); the Canadian Dakota by Wallis (1919); and the Blackfeet by Wissler (1918). While various aspects of the Sun dance are noted in these works— primarily the preparatory rituals, construction of the dance lodge, description of costuming and paraphernalia, self-torture (where applicable), and miscellaneous related ceremonies—little mention is made of the music. Densmore analyzed a minimum of Sun dance songs for the Standing Rock (Hunkpapa) (1918:99–171) and the Cheyenne and Arapaho (1936:78–82).

While ritual grammar differs from one tribe to the next, there are certain generalities common to all: (1) the initiation of the ceremony based on a vow taken by one or more persons in order to placate the deities when faced with danger on the warpath, famine, or other threat to life; (2) ritualistic construction of a special Sun dance or "medicine" lodge; (3) self-sacrifice by the participants, ranging from fasting to self-torture; (4) gazing at the sun while dancing; and (5) feasting, societal functions, and intrusive dances unrelated to the Sun dance proper.

Non-Indian viewers have been most impressed by the torture aspect of the Sun dance. Originally, dancers were skewered through the chest and suspended by rawhide ropes from a framework of poles until the flesh tore loose. Often comrades assisted by pulling the dancers backwards to hasten the ordeal. Other participants attached buffalo skulls to their shoulders and dragged them through the Sun dance camp. Children were often encouraged to jump and ride on the skulls to expedite the sacrifice. In many instances, however, dancers remained in sacrificial positions for long hours. The Sun dance period was also a time when women offered bits of flesh from their arms, and medicine men pierced the ears of children.

Compared with the total number of rituals performed at the Sun dance, the torture was relatively minimal and few men and women participated. More emphasis was placed on fasting, prayer, dancing in place, "gazing at the sun" (the Lakota term for the dance), aspiring to receive visions, and the socializing that followed the ceremonial ordeal. Through missionary appeal torture and all forms of sacrifice were prohibited by the federal government in the 1880s, but the Sun dance continued in an abbreviated form. In 1959 several tribes, notably the Oglala and Rosebud of South Dakota and the Turtle Mountain Plains Ojibwa of North Dakota, under the sanction of their respective tribal councils (and relative indifference of the federal government), resumed a modified version of the torture. Buffalo skulls were dragged at Turtle Mountain; chest piercing was continued at Pine Ridge and Rosebud.

The reinstitution of the torture has been viewed with some am-
bivalence by conservative members of the tribe. On some reservations it appears that the Sun dance is being used to attract tourists.
The dancers themselves are conservatives, but the event is admin-
istered by the tribal council. The dancers are sincere, but the usual
schism between conservative and progressive exists: the former
criticize the latter for not knowing how to conduct the Sun dance
ritual properly. Most Northern Plains tribes agree that the Arapahoe
version is the most "authentic" despite the fact that the Arapahoe
have not resumed the torture. The film *Okan: Sun Dance of the
Blackfoot,* which I reviewed (1967), reveals that the Canadian Blackfeet have retained many of the older rituals, especially the societal
ceremonies no longer practiced by the majority of tribes living in the
United States.

The Sun dance songs of the Crow and Northern Cheyenne reviewed here are parenthetically subtitled *A Dance of Thirst.* The
subtitle is somewhat misleading. Although fasting always has been
an integral part of the dance, these songs are more rightly called
"dance" songs (as opposed to prayer songs, society songs, and other
miscellaneous songs used in preparation of the dancers, paraphernalia, and dance lodge). These songs accompany the portion of the
dance which takes place inside the medicine lodge and are seven in
number for both tribes. This coincides with the seven dance songs
currently sung by the Pine Ridge and Rosebud Lakota, and also with
the number of dance songs recorded by Densmore for the Hunkpapa. The Crow songs are not similar to those of the Northern
Cheyenne (or Sioux), although both sound like dance songs and the
novice can easily misconstrue them for War dance songs (except for
the final cadences, which are distinct).

Although not mentioned on the label, a woman's voice may be
heard on the Crow songs. All songs are sung in vocables with a
peculiar introductory drum technique in which the singers begin
striking the drum half-time for the introductory phrase, eventually
doubling the tempo to normal dance time. An eagle bone whistle,
played by Sun dancers, is heard on the first band.

The Northern Cheyenne songs, likewise sung in vocables, begin
in the same manner as War dance songs, but all end with a drum

tremolo, a technique also employed by the Lakota in ending their songs.

The songs appearing on this album may very well be the only remaining vestige of Sun dance songs used by the Crow during their celebrations at Lodge Grass, Montana, in June and by the Northern Cheyenne at Lame Deer, Montana, in July. The reason for their predominance and popularity may be that the dance songs are sung in public and known by many, while the songs used in conjunction with miscellaneous preparatory rites are limited to participants and religious leaders. Since most of the preparatory songs are prayer songs, singers may be unwilling to record them for commercial use.

Ponca Tribal Songs by Sylvester Warrior, Albert Waters, and Lamont Brown. No. PONCA-119. Side I, seven bands; Side II, seven bands. One 12" 33-1/3 rpm disc.

Southern Plains aficionados will welcome this addition to the steadily growing corpus of Ponca music. Howard has reviewed an outstanding collection of Ponca songs by Indian House Recordings (1969:202–204). This Soundchief album complements the Indian House recording and presents an outstanding variety of songs by three noted Ponca singers, all of whom appeared on the Indian House record. The capabilities of the performers and the influence of Ponca music on the Southern Plains is discussed by Howard in his review. Those interested in a detailed analysis of the Ponca should consult Howard's "The Ponca Tribe" (1965b), which contains comprehensive sections on music and dance, and, especially, references to the Ponca contribution to Pan-Indian events throughout Oklahoma.

The first three bands of Side I, "Traditional Warriors' Songs," correspond in form to the War dance songs mentioned earlier. All three songs contain vocables only, are sung three times each with the final tail, and are examples of typical Southern Plains War dance style. Compared with the Northern Plains songs, the Ponca songs are sung in a lower register and the introductory phrases are very short—sometimes only two or three vocables comprise the lead. The drumming also is typical of Southern Plains style, the accent duple beats being placed at the midpoint of the song. The beats are usually accented three times, the first accent occurring on the utterance of the final vocable of the first cadence (C), and the next two accents falling on the repeat chorus.

Bands 4–6 of Side I are called "Original Straight Dance Contest" songs, and while they also conform to the typical War dance form, they are definitely "Ponca." Words replace the vocables in all three songs. "Straight" dancing is a slower, more dignified form of War dancing more closely related to the original "Grass dance" out of which the current War dance grew.

Band 7 contains four short songs called "Fancy Men's Championship Dance Songs" that do not correspond to what is usually considered "Fancy dance" in Oklahoma; rather, they represent a variation of Fancy dancing sometimes referred to as "Buffalo dance" or "Squat dance." While the typical Fancy dance song is nothing more than an accelerated form of the "normal" War dance, the examples on band 7 are of a binary form: each song begins with a drum tremolo that breaks into a very fast rhythm. The traditional cadence is eliminated and no tails are sung. The first three songs are sung in Ponca, while the fourth is sung in vocables only.

Though these songs are variations, they are nevertheless widely used as contest songs. During the tremolo the dancers stand, stoop, or squat, shaking their bells rapidly. As the drum moves into a rapid, steady beat, the dancers dance in traditional Fancy style, ending on the last beat of the song and drum. Since the cadence is irregular by most tribal standards of War dance songs, visitors to the Ponca are often caught off guard when dancing to the "Ruffle dance" variation. Because of the cadence anomaly, these, along with "Stop dance" songs described earlier, are sometimes referred to as "trick songs" by non-Ponca or non-Oklahoma Indians.

Side II offers still more variety of Ponca music. Band 1 begins with the traditional "Flag Song," comparable to the Indian "National Anthem" sung as a prelude to Indian events. The melody is somewhat standardized in Oklahoma, but the words are Ponca. The form of the Flag song closely resembles older songs in which the first half of the song is sung in vocables and the repeat in words.

Band 2, "Veteran's Honoring Song," and Band 3, "Memorial Song," commemorate Indians fighting in the armed services. Their form is that of the typical slow War dance song. Both songs are sung in Ponca.

Bands 4–6 are called "Trotting Dance" songs. The Trot dance songs, according to Howard (1969:203), are rare; only five survive today. The Trot dance is performed by many Northern and Southern Plains tribes under various names. In it dancers trot in time to the drum rather than perform the standard flat step associated with War dancing. In 1950 the Wichita presented their version of this dance, which they called "Horse stealing dance," at the American Indian Exposition in Anadarko, Oklahoma. The North Dakota Lakota do a variation of this called the "Stomp dance" (not to be confused with the Southeast variation), in which the dancers simply step in time to the drum while performing intricate, weaving body motions. The Southern Plains Trot dance is more reserved.

The concluding band, not listed on the label, is another typical slow War dance song sung in vocables only, three renditions and a tail.

The singing quality is excellent on this album. Cover notes would be especially valuable on a record which contains so many word-songs, for the texts themselves would add valuable insight into a tribe which wields so much influence over the music of the Southern Plains.

Comanche Peyote Ritual Songs by Nelson Big Bow. No. COMANCHE-591. Side I, seven bands; Side II, six bands. One 12" 33-1/3 rpm disc.

Kiowa Peyote Ritual Songs by Edward Humming Bird. No. KIOWA-590. Side I, seven bands; Side II, eight bands. One 12" 33-1/3 rpm disc.

The Kiowa and Comanche songs presented here are typical of the ritual music performed at meetings of the Native American Church. The Native American Church, incorporated in 1918, claims a membership of 225,000 Indians from tribes ranging from Mexico to Canada.[3] The degree to which Peyotism influences tribes is debatable. The church's stronghold is Oklahoma, but Peyotism may be found on practically all Plains reservations and, to a lesser degree, in the Southwest among a few Pueblos. Normally there is less Peyotism among tribes which still adhere to tribal religions, though many tribes are beginning to compromise their religious adherence and it is not uncommon on some reservations to find persons active in Christian, Peyote, and tribal religions at the same time (cf. Powers 1987).[4]

It is difficult to determine just how "Kiowa" or "Comanche" the songs presented here really are. Peyote songs are widely diffused throughout the northern American continent. The songs on these albums, with the exception of *Comanche,* Side I, band 3, which has words, are comprised entirely of vocables ending with the characteristic cadential formula *he na yo we* (or variations). Although only one singer is mentioned on each album, he is joined by one or two voices. The accompaniment is the traditional water drum and gourd rattle. The songs, which are evidently "personal" songs (the standardized opening song is missing from both albums) are valuable to the student of music diffusion in the Native American Church.

Kiowa Black Leg Warriors Society (Ceremonial Dance) by Kiowa Tribal Singers, Oklahoma. No. KIOWA-385. Side I, six bands; Side II, six bands. One 12 " 33-1/3 rpm disc.

Early investigators of the Kiowa, namely Mooney (1896) and Lowie (1916), both refer to the society whose songs appear on this recording. Lowie called the society "Black Feet," while Mooney translated it "Black Leg." Harrington (1928:189) also translates the same "Black Leg" (*tou-k'ougyH-kiH*). According to Lowie (1916b: 846–847), the Black Leg had two leaders. One carried a crooked lance covered with beaver skin and eagle feathers. As in societies among other Plains tribes, this stick was planted in the ground during battle and the owner was expected to hold his ground, no matter what the odds, until a comrade released the stick for him. The Black Leg Society, nowadays called Black Legging Society, has been revived by the Kiowa. Turley states:

> During the 1950's the Kiowa tribe was able to present a Black Legging Society dance at Anadarko. This sparked quite a bit of interest in this dance since it had not been done for quite some time. The Kiowas pooled their knowledge in attempting to reconstruct the Society as it used to be. They even consulted Mooney's early an-

thropological writings which referred to the original dance and the names of the persons involved in it. The present Society performs the Black Legging dance each November 11, Veteran's Day weekend. The Kiowa-Apache tribe also performs the revitalized Black Foot Society Dance which is similar in structure to the Kiowa dance. (1966:7)

I witnessed a Black Legging Society dance at Anadarko in August 1960 in which members wore black tights and black fringed shawls as kilts. One carried a crooked lance; all danced in a straight line, stepping in place in time to the music. During the dance, a veteran narrated his exploits in World War II over the public address system in Kiowa, which was translated by the master of ceremonies. According to my information, the present-day society is restricted to veterans.

Again due to the absence of cover notes, one is not sure whether or not the songs constitute the complete Black Legging repertory. All songs contain vocables only, and all end with the same cadential formula (except Side I, bands 1 and 2, which are similar to one another but differ from the rest). The drumming is reminiscent of Round dance drumming (slightly accented duple beats), and each set of songs ends with a drum tremolo. The songs on Side II are slightly faster than those on Side I, suggesting that the songs may be sung in some logical order. The voice quality of the group is especially pleasing to those familiar with the Southern Plains idiom, and the group is further enhanced by the presence of a woman's voice.

Collectively, the albums reviewed here are substantial contributions to American Indian music and indicate the current musical trend of the Plains Indians. All albums are highly recommended to those interested in Plains Indian music.

Chapter 9

Towards a Sound Ethnography

If English texts employed in contemporary Native American music serve as an index of acculturation, as Rhodes originally suggested (Rhodes 1963), how are we to classify Christian hymns composed and sung in native texts, fitted to traditional melodies and rhythmic patterns, which, but for the absence of percussion, might be misconstrued as a pagan paean?

Two volumes of Kiowa Church songs, recorded at Carnegie, Oklahoma, on March 31, 1971, serve as a point of departure.

Kiowa Church Songs, Vol. 1. One 12" 33-1/3 rpm disc. 1972. IH 2506. Mono. Jacket notes.

Kiowa Church Songs, Vol. 2, One 12" 33-1/3 rpm disc. 1974. IH 2507. Mono. Jacket notes.

According to the brief jacket notes, several hundred similar songs are sung by Baptists and Methodists, who prefer to sing their hymns slowly and unaccompanied, and by Pentecostals, who prefer singing faster and to the accompaniment of drums and tambourines. Percussion is absent in these recordings in order to ensure clarity of texts. The singers featured on these volumes are members of the Pentecostal Church and include David Apekaum, Ray Cozad, Harry Domebo, Walter Geionety, Tom Tointigh, Ruby Beaver, Kathleen Redbone, Joyce Robinson, and Nancy Tointigh.

The same photograph of the singers appears on both covers, as does a photo of the Kiowa Indian Pentecostal Church. Since the two volumes exist as a set, it would have been more interesting and informative to have had a variety of photos rather than the present duplication. As a source of future historical research it would also be useful to have left-to-right captions of the singers' names rather than a list in which, for some reason, males are alphabetically segregated from similarly alphabetized females.

Volume I contains 10 songs on Side I and 12 on side II. Volume II contains nine songs on each side. All of the songs were composed, and are rendered in, the Kiowa language. Free translations of the texts, interpreted by David Apekaum, are noted. An abbreviated, uncritical history of how Christianity reached the Kiowas appears on each album.

The melodies and performance style of Kiowa Church music is quite reminiscent of traditional, non-Christian songs. Rhodes earlier noted:

> The Kiowa have been taught hymns and gospel songs in their native language to the traditional Euro-American tunes, but unlike most other tribes they have maintained their tribal identity and found their religious satisfaction in hymns of their own making. Though the words are little more than a translation of a simple Christian sentiment into the Kiowa language, the melodies are original and thoroughly Indian in style. (Rhodes 1960:326–327)

Like the traditional singing of War dance songs and other genres, a leader begins each of the Church songs and is then joined by the remainder of the chorus. Melodic lines cascade in a predictable Plains manner, but there is perhaps less vocal tension and quavering than in traditional Kiowa music. Although not stated in the notes, it would be interesting to know if Church songs are freely borrowed from other genres of Kiowa music, since this process of intergeneric borrowing seems to hold for the Kiowa as well as other Plains music. It would also be instructive to know who composes the songs, inasmuch as Rhodes is quite clear that "Many of the most beloved hymns of the Kiowa have been made by women" (ibid.:329).

Without more information than the notes offer us, questions arise. The music itself does not answer many of the most intriguing ones, which must be dealt with critically. If these Church songs are, like the English text songs, indexes of acculturation, just what or who is to be acculturated? In which direction should we point the acculturation arrow? Are the Kiowa truly becoming Christian, or are Christian concepts being formally adopted into Kiowa culture, partly through the medium of musical composition and song text, a process I have noted elsewhere on the Northern Plains (Powers 1977, 1986, 1987)?

The analysis of song texts, I think, would be helpful, but we are not provided with linguistic information. These songs, as Rhodes has pointed out, are not like Church songs found among other tribes. They are not simply missionary translations of Christian hymns into a local dialect. In fact these songs, compared with what has been published on other tribal hymns, are indeed unique, and might hold a clue not only to the process of composition but also to the process of conversion, if in fact conversion, as we usually understand it, is occurring.

As it stands, we are given free translations of texts, but the translations are not necessarily typical of the Christian sentiments that Rhodes speaks about. Of the total of 40 songs, the concepts of happiness, mind, and trouble, over which Christianity holds no monopoly, appear in 30. For example:

I prayed to God,
And He made me feel happy in my mind
And I'm happy continually. (I [1]:5)

It's God that made me feel happy in my mind
And I'm happy hereafter. (I[1]:6)

I am very thankful God made me feel good in my mind.
(I[1]:8)

He is the true spirit in your mind
And He knows how to make you happy. (I[2]:3)

God, You take me out of many troubles,
For that reason, I'm happy in my mind. (I[2]:5)

Through prayers, it makes me happy.
I like the prayers, it makes me happy. (II[1]:5)

Jesus' words makes me happy
It makes me very happy. (II[2]:6)

If we can set aside poor grammar or uncolloquial free translations, the texts above, in my opinion, are not expressions of exclusively Christian sentiments. We should not be misled by glosses
(God, Jesus) if we do not have direct information about the original
Kiowa text and the manner in which "Christian" concepts are
verbalized. It is also too simple to conclude that what we are witnessing is a syncretic process, since all religions are syncretic.

The other albums considered here will help make my point. A
recording session at Lake Andes, South Dakota, on July 6, 1976,
resulted in the production of four volumes of Yankton Sioux Peyote
songs:

Yankton Sioux Peyote Songs, Vol. 1. One 12" 33-1/3 rpm disc. 1976. IH
4371. Mono. Jacket notes.
Yankton Sioux Peyote Songs, Vol. 2. One 12" 33-1/3 rpm disc. 1977. IH
4372. Mono. Jacket notes.
Yankton Sioux Peyote Songs, Vol. 3. One 12" 33-1/3 rpm disc. 1977. IH
4373. Mono. Jacket notes.
Yankton Sioux Peyote Songs, Vol. 4. One 12" 33-1/3 rpm disc. 1978. IH
4374. Mono. Jacket notes.

There is a total of 88 songs, some categorized as "straight songs"
(those sung with vocables only), while the remainder are not classified but in fact are songs composed primarily of native texts. Again,
for these latter songs, we are provided with free translations. The
singers include Joe Abdo, Jr., Quentin Brughier, Lorenzo Dion, Asa
Primeaux, Duane Shields, Joseph Shields, Sr., and Philomene Dion.

In these selections we have another variation of American Indian
music and we are confronted with another kind of Christianity:
Peyotism, which, despite the popular myth of its homogeneity, is as
diverse as Protestant denominations, its major schism (Half Moon
and Cross Fire rites) complicated by multitudinous tribal variations.

The Yankton songs are interesting from a cross-tribal perspective
because, unlike most Peyote songs, a number are sung in the native
language, Dakota. More unusually, some are sung in harmony. The
addition of harmonic lines is attributed to an influence from Lakota
of the Crow Creek reservation who belong to Presbyterian or Episco-
pal congregations and, according to the jacket notes, learned harmo-

nic singing in the course of learning hymns of their denominations. It was later adapted to Peyote music at Greenwood, South Dakota.

I do not know how faithful the Kiowa free translations are to the original texts, but the translations of Dakota quite frequently miss the mark. This is presumably due to the fact that the translations are simply accepted and recorded uncritically. In the process, the meter and meaning of the text are sheared away, and only the crudest skeleton of the esthetic form remains. This of course is not the fault nor the responsibility of the translator, and we are well aware that among all societies translation is both an art and a science which requires more than merely being a native speaker of the language. As an example of an inadequate text and its corresponding translation, consider the following from Volume I, Side 2, Band 2:

Wacekiya yo yo yo
Wacekiya yo yo yo
Wacekiya yo yo yo
Wacekiya yo yo yo
Wacekiya yo Ho yani kte he ya na he ye yo we
Maȟpiya kin heciya ya ya wiconi ye ye (haya hana yo)
Wacekiya yo Ho yani kte he ya na he ye yo we

Pray! yo yo yo
Pray! yo yo yo
Pray! yo yo yo
Pray! yo yo yo
Pray! Ho, you will live he ya na he ye yo we
There in heaven ya ya, there is life ye ye (haya hana yo)
Pray! Ho, you will live he ya na he ye yo we.

This is my translation and transcription from the record; underlined parts represent vocables. The parenthetical sections of vocables were not entirely clear to me.

The free translation given on the cover is:

Pray, you're going to live.
There's life in Heaven.

Even without hearing the music, I believe the above example indicates a great deal of melodic and linguistic intricacy which does not appear in the sparse cover liners. And here I am consciously echoing

Sheehy's criticism of the "frequent lack of adequate written documentation to accompany records" (Sheehy 1979:354). I also commiserate with the arguments that extensive notes decrease public appeal, and at the same time are economically prohibitive. But Sheehy also offers a solution in the acquisition of special funds from public and private agencies.

There is still another reason why some record companies do not provide extensive historical or cultural information, which has to do with the nature of their production goals, that is, they produce recordings for the "Indian" market, which presumably does not require scholarly exegesis. This argument implies that the recordings are for listeners who already know the music, and simply want to collect it either for their listening pleasure or perhaps to learn the songs. However, this argument rules out the fact that Native Americans are also scholars and have an esthetic interest in the recordings. It also implies that only Kiowas buy Kiowa records, or Lakota, Lakota records, and so on, which according to my experience is simply not the case. If this were true, free translations would be unnecessary. Furthermore, with the proliferation of Native American Studies programs both on and off the reservation, it would appear that more exhaustive documentation would provide a welcome support for these ongoing programs.

The recording companies specializing in Native American music have provided a considerable service to scholarship over the past years, and my comments in no way detract from the high esteem I have for their skills and perseverance. We have seen great improvements in recording techniques and fidelity as well as in the depth of their scope. But if we are to achieve a more sophisticated sound ethnography, we should seek means to include much more ethnographic, historical, biographical, and musical information along with the sound recording.

Kiowa Gourd Dance, Vols. 1 and 2. Recorded at Carnegie, Oklahoma, June 10, 1974, by Tony Isaacs. Two 12" 33-1/3 rpm discs. 1975. Indian House IH 2503–2504. Jacket notes by Tony Isaacs.

The persistence of Native American values is best understood not as an *adherence to* old traditions but, rather, a *reinvention of* old traditions. New content is molded into old forms in structurally predictable ways. Like Lévi-Strauss's *bricoleur,*[1] contemporary Indian song- and dance-makers work with a finite set of musical and choreographic materials which are constantly torn apart and rebuilt in culturally meaningful and relevant ways. *Kiowa Gourd Dance* is reflective of this process, one which reinvigorates old music and dance with new significance.

The Gourd dance was traditionally performed by the Kiowa Tai-pe-go Society at annual Sun dances. When the Sun dance was prohibited by the U.S. government in 1890, the Gourd dance continued to be performed until 1927, when the last of the Tai-pe-go died. It was informally reinstated on Armistice Day, 1946. In September 1956, descendants of the society members reorganized. Since then the Gourd dance has become a popular secular dance not only of the Kiowa but also of most of the tribes on the Southern and Northern Plains.

The two Indian House volumes are timely inasmuch as James H. Howard regards the Gourd dance as a burgeoning form of revitalization movement (Howard 1976). He shows how the dance has grown from an occasional powwow "filler" in Oklahoma during the 1950s to a full-fledged ceremony in its own right in the 1970s—one which can now be found not only in Oklahoma but also on the Northern Plains.

The two volumes contain a total of 23 songs, recorded with traditional Indian House technical excellence, and the jacket notes by Tony Isaacs are instructive. Many of the songs are commented on by Leonard Cozad, Sr., one of the 12 male and female singers featured on the recordings. While some bands are simply labeled "Gourd Song," others are more elaborately discussed. Cozad says about one song:

> Where everybody is in the mood, and when they sing this fast song—I would put it this way, it's like an attacking—attacking an enemy and all of that, and it makes them build where they want to go right on to the skirmishes. Original gourd song. Right speed, that's the way it's supposed to sound.

The unedited comments are appropriate and underscore the exciting and dynamic quality of the Gourd songs. There are unexpected changes in the volume of the voices and drum, and melodic lines are forcefully interrupted by men shouting and the chilling ululations of the female singers. In the background, five men are dancing, keeping in time to the large bass drum by shaking rattles— now made from baking powder cans and metal salt shakers but once fashioned from gourds and rawhide.

Objectively, the dance itself is not as spectacular as Fancy or Straight dancing. Men are dressed in mufti except for blue and red trade blankets, Peyote-style jewelry, and mescal bean bandoliers. The men form a line on the outer periphery of the dance area, bobbing up and down and shaking their rattles in time to the music. During specific parts of the song, the line advances toward the centrally located drum and singers. As each song in a set of eight ends, the drum strikes a tremolo, and the dancers shake their rattles accordingly. Women dance but remain along the outer periphery. After a full set of songs has been sung, the dancers return to their seats and are given water. Sets are often interspersed with give-aways and other specialty dances.

These volumes complement two others, one recorded by Canyon (Boley 1973) and an earlier collection by Ethnic Folkways (Thornton 1964). The latter has a type of Gourd song, not included in the Indian House recordings, in which the songs are interrupted by the sound of a cavalry bugler, the origin of which is attributed to a historic battle in which a bugler was captured by the Kiowas and required to play "Charge" or be killed. The tradition was carried on until recent times by soldiers at Fort Sill, Oklahoma (Howard 1976; Rhoades 1970; Thornton 1964).

Earlier references to the Gourd dance society are found in some anthropological works (Lowie 1916b; Mooney 1896, 1910). Harrington glosses the name of the Tai-pe-go society (THepei-ga) as "name of a Kiowa order . . . skunkberry man" (Harrington 1928: 162), the meaning of which has been lost.

The recordings were made live at Carnegie, Oklahoma, where most Kiowa live today. We are fortunate that Tony Isaacs and Indian House have made *Kiowa Gourd Dance* available to an audience which would otherwise not be aware of this particularly significant music and dance of contemporary Indian America.

War Dance Songs of the Kiowa, Vol. 1. O-ho-mah Lodge Singers. One
    12" 33-1/3 rpm disc. 1976. Indian House IH 2508. Jacket notes by
    Tony Isaacs.
War Dance Songs of the Kiowa, Vol. 2. O-ho-mah Lodge Singers. One
    12" 33-1/3 rpm disc. 1976. Indian House IH 2509. Jacket notes by
    Tony Isaacs.

The rapid diffusion of the Grass dance complex, forerunner of
contemporary powwows, inspired a majority of Plains tribes to
incorporate many musical and choreographic features of the Pawnee prototype into the framework of older existing institutions
(Powers 1971:104–108). These "dance" or "feast" associations,
along with "head man" and "warrior" sodalities, were reported
widely in the well-known *Anthropological Papers* of the American
Museum of Natural History (e.g., Lowie 1916b for the Kiowa; but
see also Howard 1976; Mishkin 1940). The present songs are identified with the Kiowa variant, a society whose name was somehow
ignored in the *Papers* but referred to by Harrington (1928:126) as
"ou-hou-ma-kuan (ou-hou-ma, unexplained; *kuan* 'to dance')."
    The society was first investigated by Gamble (1952), who calls it
the "O-ho-mo Society" and suggests that "in other tribes this lodge
is known as the Omaha dance" (ibid.: 97). Gamble believes that the
Kiowa term is a corruption of the tribal name Omaha, which is also
found as a societal name among the Oglala (Wissler 1912:48–52).
Gamble's conclusion seems logical inasmuch as the components of
the Kiowa version are similar to those of the Lakota and other Plains
tribes such as the Cheyenne, from whom the Kiowa received the
dance around 1880. More recently, Laubin and Laubin made brief
reference to the "O'homo Dance," noting that "the last time the full
ritual was given was in 1922" (1977:470). In 1949, however, Gamble was adopted into the Lodge, and listed their dances as "O-ho-
mo Society dance; Starting dance; Whistle man's dance; Initiate's
dance; Song owner's dance; and Give away dance" (1952:100–
101). He states that prior to 1900 other dances were performed,
namely, the New Wearer of the Tail Piece dance (the "crow belt" or
"bustle" worn by the leader); Tagging dance; and Adoption dance.
The Laubins' claim, then, must be challenged seriously and at-

tributed to their misguided philosophy, which states that only until 1911 were there "plenty of 'real Indians' alive" (1977:454).

Isaacs refers to the Lodge as "O-ho-mah," phonetically nearer to Harrington, and translates it "war dance." But clearly Harrington is correct, and the translation is properly "O-ho-mo (or -mah) *dance.*" The discrepancy in the final syllable is unexplained; I have heard it *ohomo,* but on one recording it is clearly pronounced *ohoma,* possibly a free or stylistic variation.

The two volumes contain a total of 38 songs. With the exception of the Starting, Squat, Trick, Contest, and Quitting songs, all are typical War dances, sung with two or three renditions plus tail. A number are personal songs of the members, each of whom is identified in the notes. Only two of the songs have texts, and they are particularly interesting when viewing the word-vocable relationship. On Vol. 1, Side 1, Band 2, a short text translated "O-ho-mah dancers, get up and dance. It's good." is interspersed between vocabalic phrases in the following manner: of three renditions plus tail, the first is sung with vocables only; in subsequent renditions, the same text appears in *each half* of the song. This may be diagrammed thus:

First rendition $A(v)B(v)C(v)B(v)C(v)$
Subsequent renditions $A(v)B(t)C(v)B(t)C(v)$

(A = introduction/second; B = theme; C = first/final cadence; v = vocables; and t = texts.) Equally interesting is a longer text (Vol. 2, Side 1, Band 7) translated thus:

I like this song. This is the one.
I am glad that I hear this song.
It is good that I still hear this song.

Here, out of four renditions plus tail, the first is comprised of vocables only, but the text appears later in such a way that the initial part of the text is fitted to the first half of the rendition, while the remaining text carries over into the second half. Diagrammatically, it is:

First rendition $A(v)B(v)C(v)B(v)C(v)$
Subsequent renditions $A(v)B(t^1)C(v)B(t^2)C(v)$

There are not enough word-songs available on the volumes to indicate whether or not this is a traditional Kiowa pattern for incorporating short and long texts, but it would be interesting to investigate further, since it would provide some clues about Southern Plains compositional methods.

The O-ho-mah Lodge Singers are exemplary performers of Southern Plains music. They are composed of Ralph Kotay, Dixon Palmer, Rusty Wahkinney, Bill Ware, Tom Ware, Truman Ware, Mac Whitehorse, Mildred Kotay, Maxine Wahkinney, Florence Whitehorse, and Lucille Whitehorse. The Wahkinneys are Comanche, and it would be useful to know just how tribally exclusive the Lodge is. Both Rusty Wahkinney and Dixon Palmer were War dance champions at the American Indian Exposition in the mid-1950s. Mac Whitehorse provides comments and translations of the songs, and two photos of the group appear on the covers.

The jacket notes contain important historic and ethnographic data. Isaacs calls the singing "unique," stating that the singers strive "to perform them in the manner in which they were originally composed." One song (Vol. 2, Side 2, Band 2) is also sung on the Northern Plains, where it was recorded by Boley (Side 1, Band 5, "Fast Sioux War Dance").[2] One cannot be certain whether the song was diffused from or to the Kiowa; perhaps both versions have a common antecedent. But since the Kiowa version is listed as a personal song, it should be easy to trace, at least in theory. Although Isaacs states that the songs "include many nuances of style specifically Kiowa," it is not certain whether he means song structure or performance style. Not all songs on these volumes exhibit the forceful attack typical of Kiowa singing (e.g., Boley 1973; Isaacs 1959; Thornton 1964).

Taken as a whole, these volumes are, again, a tribute to Indian House's choice of American Indian favorites, and make an excellent addition to a growing corpus of Kiowa music.

Chapter 10

"Sioux" Favorites

Sioux Favorites. William Horncloud, Ben Sitting Up, Frank Afraid of Horse, and singers from Pine Ridge, Rosebud, Fort Thompson, and Cheyenne River, South Dakota. Canyon Records, ARP 6059. One 33-1/3 rpm disc. Side 1, seven bands; Side 2, seven bands. Cover liners.

Canyon Records began producing Sioux[1] records in 1954 on 78 rpm discs. This album contains songs which, as the cover liner states, are "selections which our Sioux listeners have made their favorites through the years." Most of the songs originally appeared as 78's in the early years.

Refreshingly, Canyon Records does not claim to offer a "typical selection" of Sioux music. There are relatively few categories of music on this album, but the songs are essentially favorites because most are still an integral part of secular functions on Sioux reservations and will unquestionably remain so for years, if not decades, to come.

Of the singers named on the album, only William Horncloud is still living.[2] He, as well as the deceased singers, have been my personal friends since my first field trip to Pine Ridge in 1948. Horncloud was one of the key singers at Pine Ridge and served as lead singer at Sun dances, Yuwipi ceremonies, and secular pow-wows, and was often on call to travel to other reservations and intertribal events to represent his tribe. He is a respected member of the community and a popular personality on several Northern Plains reservations.

Horncloud is a singer's singer who has applied himself to his talents continuously. Those who know him—Indian or non-Indian—are forced to remark, "He really likes to sing!" Horncloud normally awakens at dawn singing; does his business, whether water-drilling or cattle-herding, to his own musical accompaniment; and he is the first one at the drum, impatiently waiting for the other singers to start the dance. He began singing as a young boy and attributes his interest in singing to the place of his birth, Potato Creek, an area on the Pine Ridge reservation which has produced a host of proficient singers.

Some mention must also be made of Frank Afraid of Horse, who died in 1962 at age 91.[3] Descended from the historically famous Little Wound and Young Man Afraid of Horse, this old-timer was known for his ability and enthusiasm for singing and dancing. Until his last days, he traveled to Sheridan, Wyoming, and Gallup, New Mexico, performing with the Sioux show group. It was unquestionably at one of these performances that the majority of the songs on this album were recorded.

Afraid of Horse was a traditionalist; he rarely spoke English, was lead singer for the older Yuwipi leaders such as the famous "Chips,"[4] and lived his entire life as an old-time Sioux. He passed the day making Indian tobacco and repairing costumes, willow backrests, and other paraphernalia. He was the first one dressed at a dance and the last one to quit, despite his age. The younger Sioux who had questions about "how it was really done" in regard to Lakota tradition inevitably went to Frank's log cabin to seek the answer. (He had a stucco house built for his children but never lived in it.) Like Horncloud, Frank spent his life singing and dancing and was never too busy or too tired to teach songs to anyone who wished to learn, or simply to sing for his own amusement.

These brief references to the singers are not made out of pure sentiment or nostalgia because of my particular relationship to them. Since these singers appear on most of the bands, one may compare their singing with some of the more recent singing. On the band featuring Horncloud, Afraid of Horse, and Sitting Up, one can be assured of listening to Sioux music as it was sung before modern

Dancer in typical dance outfit, ca. 1960s. Pine Ridge. *Courtesy of the Heritage Center, Inc.*

War dancers in typical costumes of the 1960s. Pine Ridge. *Courtesy of the Heritage Center, Inc.*

influences from other regions. One will note the sometimes faltering voice of an old man pulling against the clear falsetto of a younger singer, but this is not to say—as far as the Sioux themselves are concerned—that one is not hearing "good" Indian singing. The modern groups notably have less dissonance (there is also a recording factor), which might superficially suggest superiority in vocal presentation, but in the final analysis, the value is to be determined by the members of Sioux society who, despite dissonance, listen to these recordings as some of their "favorites."

SIDE ONE

Band 1

"Sioux National Anthem" and "Victory Song," by William Horncloud. These are two separate songs which are used to open (and close) secular events. The first, called *Tawapaha Olowan* (Flag song) in Lakota, and "Sioux National Anthem" in English, may be sung by a man or a woman, or a group, with or without drum accompaniment. It is usually sung for the raising and lowering of the American flag, and all the proprieties related to any anthem are observed by the Sioux. The general audience and dancers stand and face the flag. The singers may or may not stand, but always remove their hats when singing it. I have discussed the diffusion of the song elsewhere (Powers 1968:364–365). Here the song is sung once through, first with vocables, then with the words:

Tunkašilayapi tawapaha kin oihankešni najin kte lo
Iyohlate oyate kin wicicagin kta ca hecamon welo

The flag of the United States will fly forever
Beneath it, the people will grow, that is why I do this.

The second song, although translated "Victory Song," should not be confused with the true Victory songs (*Iwakicipi*), which are sung in honor of Indian soldiers at specific times during secular events. This song is properly called an *Akicita Olowan*, or Soldier song; and though it conforms in structure to other Soldier songs, it is textually and functionally one of a kind. During this song, only veterans dance. At the closing of the event, the flag is lowered, folded, and given to a veteran to carry during the song. The texts indicate this:

He yuha natan pe (Repeated)
Tunkašilayapi tawapaha ca he yuha natan pelo.
Lakota hokšila he ohitika ca he yuha natan pe
Tunkašilayapi tawapaha ca he yuha natan pelo.

They are carrying it, charging (repeated)
They are carrying the flag of the United States, charging.
The brave Indian boys are carrying it, charging
They are carrying the flag of the United States, charging.

The song is sung twice with words, plus a tail.

Band 2

"Sioux Flag Song," by William Horncloud. This particular Flag song predates the "National Anthem" and is rarely used today. There are actually two songs sung in sequence with no interruption in voice or drum. The rhythm is six-eight with a typical Round dance cadence. The first section of the song is sung while the sponsoring committee is selecting men to dance the Flag dance, while the second part is the music for the dance proper. The first song contains the words:

"Tunkašilayapi tawapa kin iyuškinyan icu wo"
Eya ca iwacu we
Ho ekta wacipi
Le micu we

"Rejoicedly take the United States flag"
He said this and I took it.
Ho, they're dancing toward it.
Give it back to me.

The texts make no particular sense unless one knows the structure of the dance. The men dance in pairs in a double file. The first two hold an American flag and swing it back and forth as they dance. Then they hand it to the two men directly behind them, who take the lead while the original leaders take their place at the end of the double file. Thus each pair of dancers awaiting their turn to grasp the flag are dancing "toward it." This is repeated over and over until all pairs of men have had a chance to dance with the flag. "He" in this case refers to the committeeman who selected the dancer. When the original pair again reach the head of the file, the flag is given to them and the dance is completed. The actual dance song contains vocables only and is sung as many times as is needed for each pair to dance with the flag (Powers 1962b).

Band 3

"Scouting Dance Song" by Horncloud, Sitting Up, and Afraid of Horse. In Lakota, this dance is accurately translated *Tunweya Wacipi* (Scout dance), but in English it is usually referred to as "Sneak-up dance." This dance is a vestige of a society dance (Powers 1962b) which is frequently performed by touring performers at intertribal celebrations and less frequently on the Sioux reservation. The form of the song is binary; the dancers squat or crouch in place, advancing toward an imaginary enemy during a drum tremolo, and dance rapidly toward their foe during the pulsating beat. The words are reminiscent of the war leaders who organized forays against hostile tribes and, in this case, were wounded and had to be carried home:

Le yuha manipe
(repeated during drum tremolo)
Eca blokaunta ca wašošeyape
Le yuha manipe
Le yuha manipe
Le yuha manipe

They are carrying him
Behold the warrior in the thick of battle
They are carrying him
They are carrying him
They are carrying him

Afraid of Horse leads the first part of the song. The song is sung three times; a hiatus occurs between the first two songs, and the third segues into the fourth. On the fourth song the lead switches to Horncloud. There is no tail sung for this song.

Band 4

"Chief's Honoring Song," by Horncloud, Sitting Up, and Afraid of Horse. The melody of this traditional honoring song for a leader is well known on all Sioux reservations. I have recorded a variety of texts which accompany this melody; usually the name inserted at the beginning is that of a local leader—for instance, Sitting Bull at Standing Rock, Spotted Tail at Rosebud, Red Cloud (or Crazy Horse, depending in what community one lives) at Pine Ridge. In this particular song, the name (James) Iron Cloud is inserted; thus the song was probably recorded at Gallup, since Iron Cloud was responsible for contracting the Sioux group for a number of years. The song falls under the general classification of Honoring songs (*Ic'ilowan;* "to sing for one's own"), but when it is applied to a prominent leader, it is usually translated as Chief's song. The texts are:

Mahpiya Maza Lakota mayašina
Aiyapi waun welo
Iyotiyewakiye lo.

Iron Cloud, you told me to be an Indian
They're gossiping about me.
I'm having a difficult time!

The usual form of the text at Pine Ridge is:

Mahpiya Luta Wašicun mayašina
Iyotiyewakiye lo
Oyate kin heyakeyape lo.

Red Cloud, you told me to be a white man
I'm having a difficult time!
The people said this.

Whether "Indian" or "white man" is used in the text, the obvious translation refers to the difficulty in making the transition from one culture to another after the institution of the reservation system. This song dates back to about 1880.

Band 5

"Fast Sioux War Dance," by Horncloud, Sitting Up, and Afraid of Horse. This is a song sung to the traditional "Omaha" dance and is composed of vocables only. It is of the incomplete repetition type but lacks the traditional tail that would normally end the song. It is sung through four times.

Band 6

"Korea Memorial War Song," by Horncloud, Sitting Up, and Afraid of Horse. This song is a typical Soldier song sung in honor of Indians who served in the Korean war. The words are:

Okute yaunpe
Okute yaunpe
Okute yaunpe
Koreata okute yaunpe
Lakota hokšila cannunpa yuha
Okute yaunpe
Koreata okute yaunpe.

You are shooting
You are shooting
You are shooting
You are shooting in Korea
Indian boys, carrying the pipe,
You are shooting
You are shooting in Korea.

In rendering this song, some singers replace the word *yaunpe* (you [pl.] are) with *natanpe* (they are charging), thus literally translating the phrase "They are charging as they shoot."

The structure of this particular song is similar to those related to other wars, and dates back to the mid nineteenth century, when the Sioux were fighting the Crow, Shoshoni, and other enemies. In other songs Korea is interchangeable with *Kisunla* (Japanese) or *Iya Šica* (Germans') *makoce* (land). One particular song of this structure tells of the bombing of Tokyo. In older songs, either the tribal name of the enemy or the area (e.g., *Waziyata* ["up north," i.e., against the Crow]) was used. The mention of carrying the pipe is frequent in songs of this type and may be traced back to the period when Sioux war parties traditionally carried a pipe sealed with buffalo fat into battle. If the Sioux were victorious, the seal was broken and the pipe was smoked. Carrying the pipe also has the connotation of assuming the spirit of Indianism in battle, and reflects the Sioux attitude toward the pipe in general: it is a source of power, and the universal medium of communication with the deities in all religious observances.

Band 7

"Sioux Love Song," by Horncloud, Sitting Up, and Afraid of Horse.

Šic'eciye cin, Šic'eciye cin, woie namaȟ'un we
Šic'eciye cin niye unkun teciȟ'ila waun kte
Wikoškalaka kici yaun kin toȟ'an ota slolwaye
Wikoškalaka toh'an wanice wanji kici yaun šni ye

Brother-in-law, Brother-in-law, hear my words
Brother-in-law, once we were together and I loved you
I know that the woman you're with now has a bad reputation
If she didn't, you wouldn't be with her.

SIDE TWO

Bands 1 and 6

"Rabbit Dance." Band 1 is sung by "singers from Pine Ridge, Rosebud, Ft. Thompson, and Cheyenne River," obviously referring to a mixed group of singers from the four reservations. Band 6 is sung by Horncloud, Sitting Up, and Afraid of Horse.

Both Rabbit dance songs are typical of one of the few social dances in which men and women dance together as partners. The history, diffusion, and structure of Rabbit dances have been discussed elsewhere (Powers, 1962a). Both songs contain vocables during the first half of the song, and texts in the second half. The textual segment begins with the corruption of the English word "dearie," and all texts allude to love and courtship.

In earlier Rabbit dance songs, the word *Scepanši* (cousin: a female's vocative for *FaBrDa* or *FaSiDa*) replaced "dearie," and implied that despite the fact that Rabbit songs were *sung by men* (sometimes joined by women) in chorus, the sentiments expressed in the texts were those of a *single woman*. Since Lakota women use a number of terminal particles (mostly imperative and entreaty forms, as well as interjections) which differ from those of Lakota males, the Rabbit dance songs are consistently "female" in gender when introduced by *Scepanši*. For example, where a male would normally say (or sing) *Nape mak'u wo*, "Give me your hand!" a female says *Nape mak'u we.* The latter form is used in Rabbit songs when introduced by the female vocative.

With the use of "dearie" as a vocative, the Rabbit texts are somewhat neutralized, that is, the words may express the sentiments of men or women. However, the female terminal particles are retained.[5]

The songs presented here are examples of singular Rabbit dance songs, that is, one song is repeated over and over. In the course of a dance, however, several Rabbit songs are sung—three or four renditions of one song segue into another. Possibly three separate songs may be thus linked together. Whenever the leader of the song decides to change to another, he places his hand (the hand not holding the drumstick) in front of his body palm down, then turns the palm up. This gesture signifies "change it" to the other singers. Sometimes the gesture is accompanied by the command *Yaaptan yo!*, literally "turn it over."

The Sioux call this *pawankiye,* literally "to push the voice upwards," which implies raising the register. The word also is used to express the "seconding" of the lead singer. The only thing atypical of the second Rabbit song on the recording is the absence of the tail which normally is sung during the course of an actual dance.

The first song on Band 1 refers to a woman bemoaning the fact that her sweetheart is being chased by the police, which causes "her heart to pound." The words go:

Dearie, hecamin šni yunkan
Canksa yuha wan onicuwakiya ca
Canteamayanpe

Dearie, I'd never have thought
But the policeman was chasing you
It made my heart pound.

Due to an unclear recording, I was not able to translate Band 6.

Bands 2–5

"Omaha and Grass Dance Songs" by singers from Pine Ridge, Rosebud, Ft. Thompson, and Cheyenne River. These are typical "War dance" songs popular on the Sioux reservations today. More than likely all songs on these bands were recorded at the same time at an outdoor event. Each song characteristically has three renditions and ends with a tail. Only vocables are used.

Band 7

"Love Song" by William Horncloud. Both Love songs (Sides 1 and 2, band 7), called in Lakota *Wiošte Olowan,* belong to the general class of Story songs. Love songs are always sung by men, but the stories are those told exclusively by women. As in the case of the Rabbit dance texts, the male singers use the female terminal particles.

Love songs are traditionally sung by one person with no accompaniment; however, on Side 1, Band 7, one may hear a drum. This is atypical—possibly the singer simply wanted to accompany himself; there is no apparent traditional reason. Love song melodies are interchangeable with flageolet music.

Since Love songs are sung individually, there is a greater tendency for ornamentation and deviation from a formal structure. The prototype form is ABACBA:

A = Introductory, intermediary, and final cadence
B = Theme
C = Subtheme.

The introductory cadence is eliminated from both songs on this recording but appears as intermediary and final cadences on both. The cadence is most often used to separate the theme from the subtheme, whether it is used as an introduction or a termination.

Most Love songs contain texts about jilted lovers, plays on words related to joking relationships, leaving one's lover for the military, going to jail, and so on. The sounds of the owl and coyote heard on Side 1 typically accompany Love songs when there is a group present to listen. Both the owl and the coyote in Sioux mythology are able to control certain powers over women connected with puberty and sex.

Sioux Favorites offers an interesting collection of modern and traditional Sioux music and is highly recommended.

Sioux Songs of War and Love, sung by William Horncloud. Canyon Records No. 6150. One 33-1/3 rpm disc. Side 1, seven songs; Side 5, four songs.

I first met Bill Horncloud in 1949. It was in a log cabin on the north end of Pine Ridge Village.[6] There were other singers there, all men bearing names which leaped out of the Sioux history books: Frank Afraid of Horse, Edgar Red Cloud, Francis Janis. Bill himself was a namesake of his grandfather, who had been killed at the Wounded Knee massacre.

Wherever these men gathered, there was certain to be a drum nearby. Bill's love of singing had started when he was a boy. Born in 1905 at Potato Creek in the Medicine Boot District a few miles northeast of Kyle, Bill learned to sing from the old-timers. On that memorable night the drum throbbed and I heard his voice for the first time.

It was the clear, sharp falsetto and what the Sioux call *akiš 'aš' a* (yelps) that attracted me to Bill's singing. His voice was strong, the words were clear. The night was spent listening to new songs and old songs. The songs made us laugh; some made us ponder about days gone by. Old Frank interrupted the songs to pray. He took out an old pipe, and tears streamed from his eyes as he offered it up. The mood of the evening changed to one of respect; the strength of the Sioux could be felt in the solemn beats of the drum.

That was my introduction to the songs of Bill Horncloud. Many years have passed, but the clarity and sharpness of Horncloud's singing are not forgotten. He is, as the Sioux say, *Ikce wicaša*, an old-timer, and his music reflects the values of another generation which again are being sought by younger Indian people.

It is appropriate that Canyon has offered us another album of Horncloud's songs, this time, *Songs of War and Love*. The songs express a wide range of Lakota values: the honor of a chief, the boastfulness of a warrior, and the emotions of young people in love. But these songs should not be regarded only as expressions of nostalgia. It is these excursions into the Lakota past that give meaning and substance to the Lakota present.

SIDE 1

The seven songs featured on Side 1 are old songs: songs of war journeys against the Crow and Ree, as well as against the Germans in World Wars I and II. The recent wars have given new meaning to the old songs, and because of this, the old songs survive, as do old Lakota values.

Band 1

"Honoring Song," sung by Charles Red Cloud.[7] Charles Red Cloud is the grandson of the famous Oglala chief Red Cloud, and is William Horncloud's father-in-law. This is Red Cloud's song, and the words tell of the difficulty of being Indian in a white man's world:

> *He Maȟpiya Luta*
> *He Lakota mayaši na*
> *He aiyapi waun welo*
> *He iyotiyewakiyelo*

> Red Cloud
> You told me to be Indian
> That's why people are gossiping about me
> It's so hard to do!

When the Honoring song is sung, people stand and step in place to the slow rhythm of the drum. When Red Cloud's name is mentioned, the female relatives utter the staccato cry of respect.

Band 2

"Omaha Dance Song." This is an old song composed by John Spotted Horse, one of the great singers of the reservation, who greatly influenced Bill Horncloud. Spotted Horse composed the song when he was in jail. After his death the song was sung by his brother, Robert. The words reflect the hardships of reservation life:

> *Oyate kin le wanmayankapi ye ye*
> *He miye yelo*
> *Oyate wawiyokipi k'un he miye ca*
> *Iyotiyewakiye.*

> The people used to look at me
> Me!
> The one who made the people pleased
> But now I'm having a hard time.

The song accompanies an Omaha dance.

Band 3

"War Song." This song reminisces about a warrior who went to fight against the Crow:

Kola toki le
Kola toki le
Kola toki le
Kola toki le
Kola ceyapelo
Waziyata kicizapelo
Kola toki le
Kola toki le
Kola ceyapelo.

Friend, you went away
Friend, you went away
Friend, you went away
Friend, you went away
Friend, they're crying
There was fighting up north
So friend, you went away
Friend, you went away
Friend, they are crying.

This song accompanies an Omaha dance.

Band 4

This song has been called Drum dance by some Sioux singers. The song tells about a fight with the Ree.

Tanyan makute kawinge
Tanyan makute kawinge
Tanyan makute kawingelo
Palani kin nunpa makute
Tanyan makute kawingelo

Turning back, taking a good shot at me
Turning back, taking a good shot at me
Turning back, taking a good shot at me
Two Rees—took a shot at me
Turning back, taking a good shot at me.

This song is divided into two parts, the first characterized by a drum tremolo, the second by a steady marching beat. During the first part, the dancers mill about the dance floor as if looking for enemies. In the second part, they step lively in time with the drum.

Band 5

"Omaha Dance Song." This is an old song for an Omaha dance. It is sung with no words, only meaningless vocables.

Band 6

"War Song." This song was composed to celebrate a victory over the Ree.

Palani wakute kin wau welo
Palani wakute kin wau welo
Palani wakute kin wau welo
Ceyapelo
Palani wakute kin wau welo
Ceyapelo
Palani wakute kin wau welo
Ceyapelo

I came to shoot Rees
I came to shoot Rees
I came to shoot Rees
Now, they're crying
I came to shoot Rees
Now, they're crying
I came to shoot Rees
Now, they're crying.

Band 7

"Marching Song," sung by William Horncloud. This is an old song of a warrior society which boasts of the superiority of the Sioux fighter.

The accompanying rhythm is unique among Sioux songs, and was sung while dancers marched in parades at celebrations in Gallup, New Mexico, and Sheridan, Wyoming.

Taku maka mani kokipapelo
Taku maka mani kokipapelo
Taku maka mani kokipapelo
Hoiye
Taku maka mani kokipapelo
Wahukeza wankatuya makute
Taku maka mani kokipapelo
Taku maka mani kokipapelo
Hoiye
Taku maka mani kokipapelo

They are afraid of anything that walks the earth
They are afraid of anything that walks the earth
They are afraid of anything that walks the earth
Hoiye
They are afraid of anything that walks the earth
The enemy throws his spear at me—too high!
They are afraid of anything that walks the earth
They are afraid of anything that walks the earth
Hoiye
They are afraid of anything that walks the earth.[8]

SIDE 2

Band 1

"War Song." This song celebrates the victory of the United States over the Germans in World War I and World War II.

Eyašica nata he k'un nake ceyapelo
Eyašica nate he k'un nake ceyapelo
Ceyapelo
Eyašica nata he k'un nake ceyapelo
Eyašica nata he k'un nake ceyapelo
Ceyapelo

The Germans who were charging, now they are crying
The Germans who were charging, now they are crying
They are crying
The Germans who were charging, now they are crying
The Germans who were charging, now they are crying
They are crying.

This song is sung for a Victory dance which is similar in performance to the Omaha dance.

The next four songs deal with love and courtship. The first three are Love songs (*Wioŝte Olowan*) and the fourth is a Round dance (*Naslohan Wacipi*) danced by men and women. Love is a favorite theme of songs composed after the turn of the century. Love songs are characterized by a woman bemoaning her sadness over an unsuccessful love affair. Although men always sing Love songs, they sing the words of women. Love songs are sometimes humorous, but most often they reflect the sadness of unrequited love.

Band 2

"Love Song."

> *Ociciĥe na ota cantemaŝice*
> *Ociciĥe na ota cantemaŝice*
> *Ociciĥe na ota cantemaŝice*
> *Tokanl yaun na iyotiyeyakiya ca*
> *Inayakiye cin he niye unkun kte*
> *Ociciĥe na ota cantemaŝice.*

I was no good to you, and I'm feeling so bad
I was no good to you, and I'm feeling so bad
I was no good to you, and I'm feeling so bad
So you went off but she made you suffer
If you leave her, we'll be together
I was no good to you, and I'm feeling so bad.

Band 3

"Love Song."

> *Takuwe oyaglakin na iyotiyewakiye*
> *Iyotiyewakiye*
> *Takuwe oyaglakin na iyotiyewakiye*
> *Maka akan iyecetula ŝni kin*
> *Maĥpiya iyecetu kte.*
> *Unŝimala na iyotiyekiyemayaye.*

Why do you say those things—I'm suffering
I'm suffering

Why do you say those things—I'm suffering
If I can't have you on earth
I'll have you in heaven
Pity me—you've made me suffer so.

Band 4

"Love Song."

Nioie weksuye ye
Nioie weksuye ye
Nioie weksuyelo
Waceye
Nioie weksuyelo
Waceye
Ehanni ecaš ca kici waun šni
Hecamin kin ota ye
Nioie weksuyelo
Waceye

I remember your words
I remember your words
I remember your words
And I'm crying
I remember your words
And I'm crying
It's been so long without him
How often I think about it
I remember your words
And I'm crying

Band 5

"Round Dance Song." This is an old song, sung without words. In
the Round dance, people form a circle and dance clockwise, stepping to the left, and dragging their right foot into place. Hence the
name *Naslohan wacipi* ("Dragging feet dance").

Chapter 11

Have Drum, Will Travel

Any synthesis that assesses over a century's research in limited space can only be preliminary and deficient. In cutting away the meat from the bone, there is a tendency to cut away the people from the systems and institutions to which they give substance and meaning. By way of ending this book I state what I believe to be the reason behind the overwhelming success and persistence of Plains Indian culture as manifested in music and dance.

The historical chain of events which placed American Indians in an economically and politically subordinate position has created a rearrangement of cultural content in each of the Plains tribes. Cultural institutions which were once important have disappeared, to be replaced by institutions more permissible and agreeable to the dominant white society. Music and dance are cases in point. Although religious institutions such as the Sun dance were prohibited before the turn of the century, most secular institutions maintained vitality because they did not interfere with the political and religious programs of the period—the so-called civilization programs. Perhaps as a universal feature, music and dance are permitted by dominating societies because they are believed to be quaint and harmless. Perhaps also universal is the belief that music and dance are languages—or at least dialects—of peace and understanding; they are not susceptible to hate and prejudice. Music and dance and associated material culture are thus "colorful," enabling people to express their social and cultural identities without threatening the objectives of the dominant society: they are not worthy of control or suppression.

If a shift in cultural content has occurred on the Plains—as it certainly has—then we might expect that music and dance are performed more frequently today than they were 200 years ago. We might also assume that the roles of the singers, dancers, song-makers, and performers have proliferated and have become perhaps more important in maintaining social and cultural identity. As long as such proliferation continues, American Indian people will survive despite overwhelming odds.

What we are witnessing today in the form of tribal and intertribal events is not so much a revival or a revitalization as it is a *vitalization* of American Indian culture. Had it been the lot of American Indians to decide the fate of each of their institutions, they might have decided to reinstitute a dance or society, or to participate in a ceremony deemed dysfunctional at an earlier period: such reinstitutions would indeed be cases of revival. But this is clearly not the general case in the United States. American Indians were consciously denied participation in certain aspects of their cultures, which were only later (particularly after the Indian Reorganization Act of 1934) reinstated and stamped permissible by the federal government.

Vitalization rather than revitalization was the outcome of such federal legislation. Instead of reinventing cultural institutions, Indians simply began to "catch up" on those aspects of their cultures which had been discouraged. Not enough time had elapsed for them to be entirely forgotten, and the renewal of interest was less a resurgence than a response to federal permission to resume participation in events which had always held meaning for them.

The continuing approval by government authorities of what were perceived to be relatively harmless cultural expressions was enhanced by the introduction of various programs of the Bureau of Indian Affairs designed to draw tourists to the Indian reservations. "Colorful Indian dances," which abounded on the reservations, were an important attraction. When this was coupled with what every schoolchild knows best—that *the* Indian was essentially a *Plains* Indian—even non-Plains groups began to accept the Plains powwow with its concomitant music and dance forms as the domi-

Victory celebration at Pine Ridge, South Dakota, September 14, 1945.
From left to right: Mrs. Red Bear, Mrs. Rose Eccofy, William Spotted
Crow, unidentified soldier, William Fire Thunder. *Courtesy of the Smithsonian
Office of Anthropology, Bureau of American Ethnology Collection.*

nant symbol of Indian identity, an episodic form of nationalism
which became supportive of later American Indian political movements.

What was not anticipated by federal or state programs was that
tribal secular music and dance had a peculiar feedback relationship
with tribal institutions, serving as a bridge between the white world
and the distinct cultures of the tribes. As permission to participate in
this safe (if not economically progressive) aspect of Indian culture

grew, the freedom to be Indian began to be increasingly manifested in other secular and religious spheres.

American Indians, the last to be counted in federal affairs and legislation, certainly had taken the lead when, in the 1960s, sociologists proclaimed that the melting pot theory was invalid. The essence of ethnic identity was a clear reality among American Indians long before social science discovered it.

Furthermore, music and dance, which had originally been integrated into virtually all tribal institutions, began to turn in on themselves once those institutions no longer were viable. Music and dance, once reflective of religion, politics, economics, and other aspects of Plains societies, now became a category unto itself; accordingly, singers and dancers were elevated to a new status, one not only highly symbolic of the continuation of American Indian cultures but also acceptable to non-Indian audiences. Since most of the major powwows celebrated today had their origin at the turn of the twentieth century, it is not difficult to trace many of the constituents of Plains music and dance to those institutions which were meaningful to tribes, and those which were significant to non-Indian audiences in the United States, Canada, and western Europe. The famous Wild West shows of the latter part of the nineteenth century, which partly gave rise to the notion of War dance, also created for the next century the idea of the Indian musical performer as showman. Along with this newfound role came attributes of a theatrical performer—a calendar of events, performance outside the usual setting—the rodeo arena, coliseum, auditorium, theatrical stage. And along with this new utilization of music and dance, came the idea of professionalization.

THE PROFESSIONALIZATION OF THE AMERICAN INDIAN PERFORMER

Despite all arguments for and against the degree of musical professionalization found among non-industrial societies and the inherent problems of defining the professional musician (treated aptly by Merriam [1964:123–130] and Nettl [1956:11]), the concept of professionalization can be viewed equally well as an analytical category devised by Western ethnomusicologists for the purpose of comparing other societies with their own. Professionalization *is* an important category in Western musical classification, where definitions and arguments are properly settled by professional schools, institutes, conservatories, and, most important, trade unions. One of the arguments not preferred by ethnomusicologists to date is that which states that professionalization is partly the stepchild of bureaucratization, and, as in other cultural domains in which bureaucracy plays a leading role, there is no particular correlation between professionalization and skill. As we know in our own society, the fact that a musician is paid does not ensure that a musician is particularly gifted.

In dealing with contemporary American Indian societies, the arguments over professionalization increasingly begin to fade. In some ways the analytical categories provided in the past by ethnomusicologists have given rise to what might be considered a kind of self-fulfilling prophecy: by any definition or argumentation, judging by jacket notes on most of the new recordings, American Indian singers are by Western standards becoming professionalized.

The reasons behind the emergence of an unequivocal professional singer seem clear. First, the proliferation of recording companies, beginning in the 1950s, set a number of standards which were in part an answer to the problems of the industry: the edited song, and titling of songs for the purpose of identification, a phenomenon largely unheard of before records began to be produced. Second, the arbitrary classification of songs on the basis of generalizations ("American Indian Music"), regionalization ("Northwest Coast Music"), tribal ("Kiowa Music"), and, finally, a concentration of song groups and individuals (e.g., "William Horn Cloud Sings Rabbit Songs"). Third, much of Western musical technology became available to American Indian singers—for instance, public address systems, commercially manufactured drums, and tape recorders, all of which are part of the baggage carried by traveling song groups whose reputations are known far beyond the musical arenas of their respective reservations and communities.[1]

A great change in the nature of the song group has occurred since the 1950s. The major innovation is the naming of song groups themselves. Prior to the 1950s song groups coalesced on the basis of a common place of birth (e.g., Porcupine [District] Singers) or a shared kinship (Red Cloud Singers); singers simply sang together in the same locale. Often singers from different regions of the same reservation traveled to meet and sing at dance grounds far removed from their respective homes, as if the drum itself became a hangout for friends from different neighborhoods.

Today, song groups on the Plains are more predictable and more stable. It is as if members of a group have signed exclusive contracts with their song leaders. Their store-bought bass drums are emblazoned with their group names: Red Earth Singers, Oglala Juniors, Sioux Travelers, Badlands Singers. And their group names adorn posters that advertise powwows because "name" attractions will guarantee a successful turnout of dancers and spectators.

Furthermore, their professional talents are recognized through prizes and giveaways. There are now contests for singers and their groups, as well as for dancers. In 1976, the top prize for singers brought $800.00 per drum at Pine Ridge. In 1989, it was $3,000.00. In addition to prizes, song groups are frequently paid per diem (also known as "day money," a rodeo term), salaries, and, of course, travel expenses.

Another sure sign of professionalism is the number of recordings each song group has in circulation. In some respects, like American society at large, the recording guarantees prominence and an increased number of engagements, particularly away from the home community.

But the creation of a new generation of professionalized singers, however determined, does not necessarily mean that the songs and dances do not reflect an older culture, even though certainly some modifications of both have occurred over time.

For example, in the recordings of the Ashland Singers (Daniel Foote, LaForce Lonebear, Henry Sioux, Corlett Teeth, Harvey Whiteman, and Oran C. and Wesley Wolfback), Cheyennes from Montana who formed their group in 1971, the singers demonstrate that the new professionalization does not mean conforming to the younger song style from Canada and North Dakota. Their songs continue to be sung rather traditionally, a performance style reminiscent of the early 1950s.[2]

On the other hand, the Badlands Singers, who are perhaps one of the best-known groups, sing music quite typical of the so-called

Northern style common to Montana, North Dakota, and the Canadian Plains. This is still a relatively young group which, after singing together for only two years, won three prestigious singing championships at the International Singing Contest in Bismarck, North Dakota, in 1974 and 1975. Later they were named the host drum at the twenty-fourth Oil Discovery Days at Poplar, Montana.

The Badlands Singers are from Brockton, Montana, which is on the Fort Peck Assiniboine-Sioux reservation. The singers are Roy A. Azure III, Mathew Big Fork, Russell Denny, Gary Drum, Ben Gray Hawk, Gerald R. Lambert, Adrian Spotted Bird, and Leland Spotted Bird. It is not unusual to hear their albums played in Indian homes, and they are perhaps symbolic of the young generation of powwow singers.

On the Southern Plains, where it always has been anticipated that tribal distinctions were bound to break down, we still find uniquely tribal singing. The Ponca have always been highly regarded by other Oklahoma tribes as being one of the finest groups known for their ability to remember and sing old Straight dance songs.

Much musical information is passed down from one generation to the next within the same family. For example, the lead singer for the Kiowa drum, Bill Koomsa, Sr., is a household name of the Southern Plains. He was partly responsible for the Gourd dance revival of 1941. He is the son of Bob Koomsa, likewise a prominent Kiowa singer, who was one of a committee to adopt the Kiowa Flag song after World War I.

Perhaps the most significant change in the constitution of drums has been in the establishment of intertribal drums (or "international," as some groups prefer to call themselves, since on the Northern Plains the singers frequently come from Canada as well as the United States). While some singers were always in demand to sing around the drum even when they were from different tribes, today many singers meet off the reservation in cities and decide to form a group.

For example, the Red Earth Singers, formed in Bismarck, North Dakota, in 1975, are composed of singers from the Meskwaki, Chippewa, Pottawatomie, and Cree tribes. The core of the group includes Edward Bearheart, Keith Davenport, Adrian and Wayne Pushetonequa and Dean Whitebreast. All of the members sang with other groups before meeting in Minneapolis, where they attended various colleges.

Perhaps another point can be made about the professionalization of Native American singers. Since the 1970s, there has been a tendency on the part of recording companies to present increasing numbers of songs from the same genre, such as War dance, Owl dance, and *Kahomni*. Before the Native American singer reached his recently incontrovertible status of professional, earlier records usually promised "typical" surveys of regional or tribal songs. Part of the professionalization process seems to require a focus on group style and individual renditions of the same song, a transition perhaps bolstered by the bureaucratic tendency to replace the anonymity associated with cooperative societies with the idea of individualization found in competitive ones.

What about the future of Plains Indian music and dance? I think that it is safe to say that musical performance will continue to grow. This is partly due to the fact that music and dance continue to be handed down to the younger generation. Grandparents and parents still love to see their grandchildren and children out in the dance arena. Children can even learn about singing and dancing in school, and the very same federal, parochial, and private schools that once eschewed the idea of teaching children about their "pagan" dances today sponsor active powwow clubs and performance groups.

Plains-style performance has become the ideal model for Indian celebrations all over the United States and Canada even where strong tribal ceremonies are still intact. Those ideals which are significant to American Indians—sovereignty, tribalism, and cultural and linguistic diversity—are made available to a much larger non-Indian audience through an entertainment mode than through history and politics. Television and movies still tend to do a disservice to Indian culture, although certainly there have been some improvements.

Perhaps the best hope for the future of musical performance is simply the interest and enthusiasm American Indian people have for their own culture. In April 1989, I was fortunate to take part in a symposium called "The Significance of Native American Music." What was unique about this symposium is that it was organized entirely by American Indians under the leadership of Ray Young

Getting ready for a tiny tot contest. Potowatomi powwow at Hays, Kansas. *Photo by W. R. "Doc" Wilson. Courtesy of Powwow Trails.*

Bear, a singer and poet, and was held in his local community, the Tama Indian Settlement in Tama, Iowa.

Despite the fact that Tama is a relatively small and isolated community, the academic sessions each morning were attended by a full house, as were the dances held every evening. The Meskwaki were gracious hosts and provided the right background for this unique combination of symposium and performance. But most inspiring was the fact that out of the 600 Meskwaki who live on the settlement, a majority of them, judging by the numbers of singers and dancers, were sincerely interested in musical performance. Most striking was the fact that there were seven Meskwaki drums present, each numbering about a dozen singers. One drum was made up entirely of young boys, the oldest being the leader, who was 14. Certainly this small community demonstrated adequately that native culture is alive and well in the center of the Plains.

Music and dance still serve, as in the past, to maintain distance from the otherwise unavoidable white man's world. Singers still speak in song of things unmentionable in ordinary discourse, and dancers strut before their captive audience in a manner distinctly Indian. The white world is on the horizon, but in the dance arbor the singers shout courage to the dancers and onlookers:

"Dancers, yell and dance!
For each day death is coming."
I said this, and laughed heartily.
(Lakota Omaha Dance song)

Notes to Chapters

Chapter 1
The Future Study of American Indian Music

   This is a revision of a paper presented at the twenty-fifth anniversary of the Society for Ethnomusicology in a symposium which I organized and chaired, "Native American Music: Retrospect and Prospect." The celebration was saddened by the news that Professor Alan Merriam, one of the founders of the society and one of its strongest leaders, had died in an airplane accident over Poland en route to the international musicological meetings. The symposium, and this chapter, are dedicated to his memory.

   1. By this I mean "powwow" music and dance, which will be discussed in some detail. When one speaks of powwow, one implies the Pan-Plains elements that make up most of the constituent elements of the institution. Similarly, although logically it need not be the case, "Pan-Indianism" refers mainly to the same Pan-Plains elements found in various public events. Pan-Indianism has never been adequately explained, as I demonstrate in Chapter 7.

   2. It should be noted here that at the time that this paper was first presented, James H. Howard was a participant in the symposium and gave a state-of-the-art address on the subject of Pan-Indianism. He later died after a short illness. Because both of us worked on the Plains and had similar backgrounds and interests even before becoming anthropologists, we frequently feuded over what in retrospect were minor details of Plains Indian music and dance. However, outside of professional disagreements we were friends. I regard James H. Howard as having made more significant contributions to Plains Indian music and dance (among other things) than anyone else, and his absence from the Plains is strongly felt. The greatest time we had together was when both of us were asked to judge the War dance contests at the Texas Indian

Hobbyist Association powwow in Lubbock in the summer of 1964. We sang together around the drum, we danced together in the dance area, and we ate together with our wonderful hosts. We had nothing to say about Indians that would have had any bearing on anthropology. And we enjoyed it.

3. The major work by Leslie White, Howard's teacher at the University of Michigan, is White 1959. For the systematic way in which acculturation studies were being considered, see the now famous memorandum written by Redfield et al. (1936) and a criticism of it by Bateson (1935) before the memorandum was published. Both are reprinted in Bohannan and Plog (1967).

4. I think that the best criticism of the acculturation school has been by Murphy, whose purpose was not to provide still another definition of acculturation but "to get rid of it" (Murphy 1964:845). His major point is that acculturation is not a special condition but, rather, a structural necessity of human social interaction.

5. Powers 1980b.

6. This is a problem which I also discuss in 1980b.

Chapter 2
Plains Music

Parts of this chapter first appeared in "Plains Indian Music and Dance," in Wood and Liberty (1980).

1. I myself began at the age of nine, studying music and dance in order to perform it. My teachers were both Indians and whites living in the St. Louis area, where I was born and grew up. Similarly, R. D. Theisz was, and still is, an active participant around the Lakota drum. James H. Howard began Indian dancing at age 12.

2. In a critique of the original version of this chapter, Howard states that I am incorrect in attributing regional styles to Fancy and Straight dancing: "There is . . . no difference whatever [sic] in singing style, or tempo, in the music for 'straight' as opposed to 'fancy' dancing. The same singers sing the same songs for both" (Howard 1981:335). But, in fact, after reviewing the critique, I must insist that my original statement is correct and can be verified easily in the field.

3. In the same review Howard called my attention to the fact that I had eliminated the Arikara and Hidatsa, which is true and an oversight on my part. However, he also states that I omitted the "Sioux of the Standing Rock and Sisseton reservations in South Dakota . . . and . . . the Omaha and Santee Dakota of Nebraska" (ibid.). But clearly what I call the North Dakota Lakota/Dakota (or South Dakota, if one wishes, since the Standing Rock reservation straddles both states) are the tribes in question. I have added "Nebraska" for clarity, but I have also seen the

Santees as typically "South Dakota." In the original version, contrary to Howard's claim, the Omaha were included as typically "Oklahoma."

Chapter 3
War Dance

Much of this chapter is based on some of my earliest fieldwork in South Dakota, beginning in 1948, and additional travels to Oklahoma in the early 1950s. Many of my insights were originally derived from the patience and understanding of my friend Robert J. Voelker, who was kind enough to take me along to Oklahoma on my first trip. It was on this trip that he courted his wife, Evelyne Wahkinney Voelker. I remember the entire Wahkinney family—Jake and Mary, Paul Thomas and Margaret, Rusty and Maxine, Amos Peewee and Leatrice, Floyd and Glenna, and Wilma and George, and all the others—with whom my wife, Marla, and I shared good times not only in Apache and Cyril, Oklahoma, but also in Lake George, New York, where many of them were employed as singers and dancers during the summer. My heart continues to be with them; and the memories of those days—the songs and dances, the Stomps around the Comanche camp at Anadarko during the fair, the recording sessions, and just plain sharing of time and space—are still as clear in my mind as if they happened yesterday.

1. Wissler (1916) provides the earliest and best description of how the Grass dance diffused throughout the Plains. See also Howard 1951.

2. The direction of the dance has been discussed by Marla N. Powers (1988).

3. Koch (1977), as mentioned earlier, provides an excellent overview of Plains Indian costuming. See also Cantanzaro and Voelker 1960; Feder 1958; Howard 1960, 1972a, 1972b; Powers 1966a, 1966b; Smith and Kroha 1972; Stewart 1970; Stewart and Smith 1973; Theisz 1974; Tucker 1969; and Ward 1969, 1970a, 1970b, 1970c). The best detailed articles on costuming have been published in the numerous "hobbyist" or "Indianist" publications (cf. W. K. Powers 1988a). For example, see Johnson 1972a, 1972b; Johnston 1968a, 1968b, 1968c; and Johnston and Johnston 1968, among others.

4. The second category is ideal. Even songs containing only words modify the words by extending their vowel qualities through a process akin to reduplication in linguistics. Also, word-songs frequently are introduced or terminated with vocabalic phrases. I have treated the subject more fully in Powers 1987.

Chapter 4
Music in Motion

1. Obviously the distinction between tribal and intertribal accounts

for many more distinctions between cultural categories than music and dance. The terms when juxtaposed also serve as a model for understanding contemporary political and economic relationships.

2. The idea of dancing with snakes is usually associated with the Hopi of Arizona, whose biannual dance is world famous. However, the serpentine form of the dance as it is performed on the Southern Plains (without snakes) is similar to the Stomp dance of the Southeast and eastern Oklahoma. For an interesting description of the Oklahoma Stomp dance, see Howard 1965a.

3. The argument over which came first, myth or ritual, is partly solved on evolutionary grounds. Since animals other than humans participate in rituals (say, courtship) but have no speech, ritual is primary to myth, the latter, by definition in anthropology, being verbalized. This is obviously antithetical to the theological argument that myth precedes ritual, that is, the word precedes the act. For an elaboration on this argument by one of its earliest proponents, see Wallace 1966.

4. Again Howard (1981:335) criticizes my association of the Hoop dance with the Southwest, himself opting for a Northern Plains origin. While there is no question that Northern Plains dancers danced with hoops in some of the early sodality functions, such as those of the Lakota Elk Dreamers, the idea of dancing *through* a hoop, and forming designs around the body with multiple hoops, is in the creative domain of the Pueblo Indians. Perhaps the greatest known Hoop dancer in the 1940s and 1950s was Tony White Cloud from Jemez, New Mexico. Not only did he travel throughout the world entertaining audiences, but he also taught members of his family and others how to do the dance. Tony danced with four hoops, but later younger dancers were to use sometimes as many as 30. In my opinion, the great number of hoops has little to do with the dexterity required to manipulate four hoops and keep them in motion throughout the duration of the dance. The more hoops a dancer uses, the more he must rely on creating designs with them. The ultimate result is quite beautiful to behold, yet the speed and agility seen in the Hoop dance of even one or two hoops is more challenging. Either way, it is this spectacular form of the Hoop dance that is associated with the Southwest Indians, but which is seen almost anywhere in the world that there are Indian performances for audiences.

Chapter 5
The Powwow

1. "Powwow" is derived from the Algonquian word *pauau*, which signifies a general curing ritual. According to the story, whites fascinated with crowds of Indians who gathered to observe a medicine man

cure his patient, later used the term to refer to any type of Indian gathering. While it generally is considered a strictly secular event, Gelo (1985) has argued convincingly that a number of elements found in the powwow, such as the invocation offered, are sacred, and become important parts of an Indian's religious life.

2. Howard, as I shall show in Chapter 7, is not the first person to employ the term "Pan-Indianism." However, his 1955 article is generally regarded as the one that generated the most interest.

3. Although the prize varies from one powwow to the next, War dance winners may receive as much as $1,000.00 for first prize. "Drums" also win prizes for the best singing. To date no serious work of a comparative nature has addressed the many ramifications of the powwow and its attendant traditions.

4. Interestingly in the early 1980s on the Northern Plains, powwows were being held more frequently in urban areas than on the reservations, where social gatherings had been all but replaced by Sun dances. This had changed somewhat toward the end of the decade, but there is no question that the largest of all the powwows are still held in Tulsa, Oklahoma City, Denver, Bismarck, and Phoenix.

Chapter 6
Pan-Indianism versus Pan-Tetonism

This chapter originally appeared under the title "Contemporary Oglala Music and Dance: Pan-Indianism versus Pan-Tetonism" in *Ethnomusicology* 12(3):352–372, 1968. It was subsequently reprinted in Nurge 1970. Although, as Chapter 7 reveals, I have come to prefer the term "intertribalism" over "Pan-Indianism," to make the comparison clearer I have retained the latter term throughout this chapter.

1. In this book, I am primarily interested in music and dance as well as related material culture. However, in the fields of religion, politics, and economics "nationalization" may apply well. Direction for these nationalizing efforts has come from national Indian organizations, the Bureau of Indian Affairs, and religious bodies, all of whose interests tend to crosscut the interests of individual tribes except to the extent that their efforts, when successful, have resulted in residual benefits to the tribes.

2. In suggesting Pan-Tetonism, I also suggest a larger Pan-Siouan group which is theoretically composed of all divisions of Lakota and Dakota. Likewise it seems reasonable to assume that there are other "pan-" groups, such as Pan-Blackfeet, in other areas where strong tribal confederacies are supported by a common language. Not only is there an interaction between Pan-Tetonism and Pan-Indianism, but also be-

tween other "pan-" groups, such as Pan-Teton and Pan-Plains or, hypothetically, Pan-Teton and, say, Pan-Blackfeet.

3. An absence of creativity in Oklahoma was originally suggested by Tony Isaacs. The assumption here, contrary to the usual notion that Oklahoma traditions were changing rapidly, is that in many ways Indians living close to each other were in fact protecting, if not cautiously guarding, against what they perceived to be the threat of Pan-Indianism, that is, the usurpation of tribally distinct traditions by other tribes or, worse, the loss of important parts of their culture. For more on the nature of Oklahoma singing, see Isaacs 1959. Even today, although somewhat changed since the revolution of the 1960s and 1970s, many new Oklahomans call Northern-type songs "Winnebago" songs, while Winnebagos living in Nebraska identify the same as "Sioux" songs, thus tracing through their nomenclature the obvious diffusion routes from North and South Dakota to Nebraska and Oklahoma.

4. There are song-makers around Pine Ridge who compose North Dakota songs.

5. Personal correspondence with James H. Howard, 1964.

6. There is a growing number of female Fancy dancers who compete on all the northern reservations and at urban powwows. They have been doing so since the early 1970s, after being exposed to the costumes and dance styles of North Dakota and Canadian women who traveled south to participate in powwows on the Pine Ridge and Rosebud reservations. Their costume today comprises a satin miniskirted dress with high-topped Crow-style buckskin boots. Costumes also include matching beadwork, particularly headbands, solid beaded yokes, hair ties, chokers, and earrings. Most noticeable is the long, fringed shawl, which is perhaps the most important article for competition. In the 1980s an increasing number of females began wearing "jingle dresses" and competed in dance contests for women wearing only that type of costume. The jingles are made from a variety of metal sources, including the lids of snuff cans. They serve as an unmistakable accompaniment to the women's vigorous steps. Both the shawl dance costume and the jingle dress are ultimately derived from the Canadian Plains and contrast sharply with the more traditional female dresses of buckskin and trade cloth. Relatively little work has been done on women's costuming and dance styles, but see Lessard 1972 and M. Powers 1986 for a description of Lakota women's dance styles. See the interesting article by Hatton (1986) on Northern Plains female song groups.

7. A description and some interesting insights about the importance of the giveaway at Rosebud appear in Grobsmith 1979, 1981a, 1981b; for the Northern Cheyenne, see Weist 1973; and for the Blackfeet and Plain Cree, see Kehoe 1980.

8. For the ritual of preparing and consuming dog and other sacred foods, see Powers and Powers 1984.

9. Theisz (1981) provides a description and translation of honor songs used by contemporary Lakota.

10. I realize that each element is not equally weighted, but simply serves as an illustrative approximation.

Chapter 7
Pan-Indianism Reconsidered

This paper was first presented to the faculty and students of the Department of Anthropology, University of Pennsylvania, in October 1978. After subsequent revisions it was presented to the members of the American Indian Workshop, European Association on American Studies, at Rome in April 1984.

1. The term "Pan-Indian" appears in Brant's discussion of Kiowa-Apache Peyotism as early as 1950, but only as an afterthought (Brant 1950:222). In retrospect, there are some obvious works other than the ones cited that should be part of the way anthropologists look at the American Indian and that provide the same kinds of predictions without the use of the term "Pan-Indian." Here I am thinking of such works as Colson 1949 and Gunther 1950. Kurath, admittedly inspired by Howard's 1955 article, did fieldwork in the same year in the Great Lakes; this resulted in her 1957 article on Pan-Indianism in that region. Also in 1957 Schusky published an article on Pan-Indianism in the eastern United States.

2. The most comprehensive treatment of American Indian songs with English lyrics is that by Gelo (1988).

3. The literature on this subject is exhaustive, but the seminal works include LaBarre 1932; McAllester 1949; Rachlin 1964; Slotkin 1956; Stewart 1980.

4. Rachlin's 1964 article on the Native American Church is also instructive.

5. I agree with Moore that the way I have treated the term "Pan-Indianism," as well as its historical synonyms, may fit his concern with the culture concept itself as ideology. Since Pan-Indianism is decidedly an American conceit, it is likely that it serves another purpose, that of establishing an independent subfield in American anthropology, which certainly its predecessor, acculturation studies, has done. According to Moore, "It would appear that scientific concepts and ideological beliefs behave in very much the same way through history. It is therefore often difficult for us to determine which scholarly ideas are part of the evolution of scientific thought and which merely suit the ideological needs of some particular period of history" (1974:537).

6. On the problem of the concept of tribe, see Helm 1968.

7. A sample of textbooks on American Indians since 1967 demonstrates adequately the extent to which the ideas of acculturation and Pan-Indianism have become integral to the study of contemporary American Indians. For example, Bohannan and Plog (1967) adopt the term "counteracculturative" to refer to native peoples who resist or react to foreign influences. Owen, Deetz, and Fisher in their popular text (1967) regard Pan-Indianism as a movement that reflects a "new and growing nationalism" including the Native American Church (1967:518). Prucha (1971) includes Vogt's original 1957 article on acculturation as presumably representative of the subject (Vogt 1967). Garbarino in one paragraph describes borrowings between tribes, concluding that "Art styles today are truly pan-Indian, with the emphasis on being *Indian,* rather than of a particular tribe" (1976:499). Prucha (1977) in his book on Indian-white relations includes a section on Pan-Indianism that cites a few unpublished dissertations. Another important textbook published the same year by Spencer, Jennings, et al. uses the term "Pan-Indianism" exclusively to refer to the Indian rights movements of the 1960s and 1970s, perhaps the only way in which the term, if acceptable, makes sense (1977:519–520, 532–533). In the third edition of Oswalt's popular text the author makes a rather sweeping statement that Pan-Indianism is a tribal resistance to assimilation in which "Indianism and Indianness have crystallized" (1978:527). Price (1978) includes the Sun dance along with the Ghost dance and Native American Church under Pan-Indianism (p. 41); he also states that when most Indians belong to one tribe in a single locale, they establish a "low level of pan-Indian ethnicity" (p. 137), clearly giving preference to the term even when there is no need for it. Hodge in a more recent text (1981) believes that Pan-Indianism is an important part of Indian life, and defines it generally as "joint activities performed by Indians outside of an overtly tribal context" (p. 530). But this could also apply to beet picking or going to a movie. But he does state that "Pan-Indian activity does not necessarily imply the weakening of tribal ties" (ibid.).

Chapter 8
Songs of the Red Man

This revised chapter was originally published as "Songs of the Red Man: New Releases from American Indian Soundchiefs" *Ethnomusicology* 14(2):358–369, 1970. Soundchiefs was an important producer of American Indian music in the 1960s.

1. One might want to compare the Kiowa voice with that of the Crow, since the two lived close together until the end of the nineteenth century and still continue to visit each other.

2. For a discussion of the relationship between vocables and the native language in which texts appear, see my "The Vocable: An Evolutionary Perspective" in Powers 1987.

3. This figure seems somewhat inflated today.

4. One should consult Gelo 1985 for the relationship between various religious options available to the present-generation Comanche growing up in Oklahoma.

Chapter 9
Toward a Sound Ethnography

This chapter comprises revisions of three discographic reviews originally published as "Kiowa Gourd Dance, Vols. I and II" (*Ethnomusicology* 20(2):403–404, 1976); "War Dance Songs of the Kiowa, Vols. I and II" (*Ethnomusicology* 22(1):206–207, 1978); and "Toward a Sound Ethnography of Native American Music" (*Ethnomusicology* 25(1):159–162, 1981).

1. For the significance of Lévi-Strauss's idea of *bricolage* and *bricoleur*, see Lévi-Strauss (1966:16–36); and Powers (1977:xviii).

2. This is the same song that appears on "Sioux Favorites" (Side 1, Band 5, "Fast War Dance") discussed in Chapter 10.

Chapter 10
"Sioux" Favorites

1. The term "Sioux" was quite acceptable when these recordings were made, and I have opted to retain it to prevent having to switch back and forth from "Sioux" to "Lakota," the latter being the preferred term today. While it is impossible to remove the term "Sioux" from the literature—there are many Lakota and whites who still have a romantic attraction to it—it should be noted that Lakota people today are consciously trying to replace the older term, which is derogatory, with Lakota.

2. Bill Horncloud was 86 years of age in 1989. In recent times he has been unable to sing in public because of a loss of hearing that unfortunately incapacitates many of the older singers. But privately, Bill still sings, and he conjures up songs that many of the younger generation have forgotten. It is fortunate that Ray Boley and Canyon records had the foresight to know good Lakota singing when they heard it, and were able to make it a part of the permanent record through recordings.

3. Frank was my adopted father. His daughters, Sadie Janis and Zona Fills the Pipe, are my sisters and are traditional women of the Lakota nation.

4. For a comment on the importance of Horn Chips, as he was better known, see my work on *Yuwipi* in Powers 1982.

5. After having given these songs more consideration over the years, it is quite evident that all Rabbit dance songs as well as Love songs are sung from the perspective of the woman. A recent work of mine makes the point much clearer (Powers 1988b).

6. At that time, Pine Ridge Village, as it is now called, was referred to either as Pine Ridge or as the Agency.

7. This is another variation of the Honor song appearing on the previous album, Side 1, Band 4.

8. A slightly different version of this song appears in Black Bear and Theisz 1976.

Chapter 11
Have Drum, Will Travel

This chapter comprises revisions of two discographic reviews originally published as "Have Drum, Will Travel: The Professionalization of Native American Singers" (*Ethnomusicology* 25(2):343–346, 1981); and "Ho hwo sju Lakota Singers, and Sounds of the Badlands Singers" (*Ethnomusicology* 21(1):163–164, 1976).

1. On modern song groups, see Hatton 1974.

2. A good sampling of the kinds of song groups and their styles of singing would include the following:

Ashland Singers, *Northern Cheyenne War Dance*. One 12" 33-1/3 rpm disc. 1974. IH 4201. Mono. Jacket notes.

The Badlands Singers, *Assiniboine-Sioux Grass Dance*. One 12" 33-1/3 rpm disc. 1974. IH 4101. Mono. Jacket notes.

Badland Singers, *Live at Bismarck*. One 12" 33-1/3 rpm disc. 1977. IH 4103. Mono. Jacket notes.

The Badland Singers at Home. One 12" 33-1/3 rpm disc. 1978. IH 4104. Mono. Jacket notes.

The Badland Singers, *Kahomine Songs*. One 12" 33-1/3 rpm disc. 1978. IH 4105. Mono. Jacket notes.

Kiowa Scalp and Victory Dance Songs. One 12" 33-1/3 rpm disc. 1977. Canyon C-6166. Mono. Jacket notes.

Old Agency Singers of the Blood Reserve, Vol. 1. One 12" 33-1/3 rpm disc. 1973 IH 4051. Mono. Jacket notes.

Old Agency Singers of the Blood Reserve, Vol. 2. One 12" 33-1/3 rpm disc. 1973. IH 4052. Mono. Jacket notes.

Red Earth Singers, *Live at Bismarck*. One 12" 33-1/3 rpm disc. 1977. IH 4501. Mono. jacket notes.

Red Earth Singers. One 12" 33-1/3 rpm disc. 1978. IH 4052. Mono. Jacket notes.

Bibliography

Ablon, Joan
  1964 "Relocated American Indians in the San Francisco Bay Area: Social Interaction and Indian Identity." *Human Organization* 24:296–304.

Bateson, Gregory
  1935 "Culture Contact and Schismogenesis." *Man* (35):178–183. (Reprinted in Bohannan and Plog 1967.)

Beard, Daniel C.
  1909 *The Boy Pioneer: Songs of Daniel Boone*. New York: Charles Scribner's Sons.

Black Bear, Ben, Sr., and R. D. Theisz
  1976 *Songs and Dances of the Lakota*. Rosebud, SD: Sinte Gleska College.

Bohannan, Paul, and Fred Plog (eds.)
  1967 *Beyond the Frontier: Social Processes and Cultural Change*. Garden City, N.Y.: Doubleday.

Boley, Raymond
  1973 *Fourteen Kiowa Gourd Dance Songs*. Canyon Record No. C-6103.

Brant, Charles S.
  1950 "Peyotism Among the Kiowa-Apache and Neighboring Tribes." *Southwestern Journal of Anthropology* 6(2):212–222.

Buttree, Julia M.
  1930 *The Rhythm of the Red Man*. New York: A. S. Barnes.

Catanzaro, Marina, and Evelyne Voelker
  1960 "Modern Oklahoma Taffeta Dress." *American Indian Hobbyist* 6(5–6):59–61.

Catlin, George
1967   O-Kee-Pa. New Haven: Yale University Press.
Colby, L. W.
1895   "The Ghost Songs of the Dakotas." *Proceedings and Collections of the Nebraska State Historical Society* ser. 2, 1:131–150.
Colson, Elizabeth
1949   "Assimilation of an American Indian Tribe." *Human Problems in British Central Africa* (8):1–13. Reprinted in Bohannan and Plog 1967.
Curtis, Natalie
1907   *The Indians' Book.* New York: Harpers.
Daniels, Robert E.
1970   "Cultural Identities Among the Oglala Sioux." *In* Ethel Nurge (ed.) *The Modern Sioux: Social Systems and Reservation Culture.* Lincoln: University of Nebraska Press.
Densmore, Frances
1916   "Music in Its Relation to the Religious Thought of the Teton Sioux." *In* F. W. Hodge (ed.), *Anthropological Essays Presented to William Henry Holmes*, pp. 67–79. Washington: J. W. Bryan.
1918   "Teton Sioux Music." *Bureau of American Ethnology, Bulletin* 61.
1923   "Mandan and Hidatsa Music." *Bureau of American Ethnology, Bulletin* 80.
1929   "Pawnee Music." *Bureau of American Ethnology, Bulletin* 93.
1936   "Cheyenne and Arapaho Music." *Southwest Museum Papers* (Los Angeles) 10.
1941   "The Study of Indian Music." *Smithsonian Institution, Annual Report for the Year Ended June 30, 1941*, pp. 527–550.
1944   "The Survival of Omaha Songs." *American Anthropologist* n.s. 46:418–420.
Dorsey, G. A.
1903   "The Arapaho Sun Dance." *Field Museum of Natural History, Anthropological Series* 4:1–228.
1905   "The Ponca Sun Dance." *Field Museum of Natural History, Anthropological Series* 7:67–88.
Eggan, Fred
1966   *The American Indian: Perspectives for the Study of Social Change.* Chicago: Aldine.
Feder, Norman
1954–   *The American Indian Hobbyist.* Los Angeles: Norman Feder.
1960
1958   "Oklahoma Fancy Dance Costume." *American Indian Hobbyist* 4:5–6.

1964 "Origin of the Oklahoma Forty-nine Dance." *Ethnomusicology* 8(3):290–294.

Feld, Steven
1974 "Linguistics and Ethnomusicology." *Ethnomusicology* 28(2): 197–217.

Fenner, Earl C.
1976 "The Gourd Dance." *Indian America* 9(2):30–33, 48–49.

Feraca, Stephen E.
1963 "Wakinyan: Contemporary Teton Dakota Religion." *Studies in Plains Anthropology and History,* vol. 2. Browning, MT: Museum of the Plains Indian.

Fletcher, Alice C.
1883 "The 'Wawan,' or Pipe Dance of the Omahas." *Peabody Museum of American Archaeology and Ethnology, Report* 16–17: 308–333.
1893 "A Study of Omaha Indian Music." *Archaeological and Ethnological Papers of the Peabody Museum* 1(5):231–382.

Gamble, John I.
1952 "Changing Patterns in Kiowa Indian Dances." *International Congress of Americanists, Proceedings* 29(2):94–104.
1967 "Changing Patterns in Kiowa Indian Dances." *In* Sol Tax (ed.), *Acculturation in the Americas.* New York: Cooper Square Publishers.

Garbarino, Merwyn S.
1976 *Native American Heritage.* Boston: Little, Brown.

Gelo, Daniel L.
1985 *Comanche Belief and Ritual.* Ann Arbor: University Microfilms.
1988 "Comanche Songs, English Lyrics, and Cultural Continuity." *European Review of Native American Studies* 2(2):3–7.

Goddard, Pliny Earle
1919a "Notes on the Sun Dance of the Sarsi." *American Museum of Natural History, Anthropological Papers* 16(4):223–270.
1919b "Notes on the Sun Dance of the Cree in Alberta." *American Museum of Natural History, Anthropological Papers* 10(4):295–310.

Grobsmith, Elizabeth S.
1979 "The Lakhota Giveaway: A System of Social Reciprocity." *Plains Anthropologist* 24(84):123–131.
1981a "The Changing Role of the Giveaway in Contemporary Lakota Life." *Plains Anthropologist* 26(91):75–79.
1981b *Lakota of the Rosebud: A Contemporary Ethnography.* New York: Holt, Rinehart and Winston.

Gunther, Erna
1950 "The Westward Movement of Some Plains Traits." *American Anthropologist* (52):175–180.

Hagan, William T.
1961 *American Indians.* Chicago: University of Chicago Press.

Hallowell, A. Irving
1957 "The Backwash of the Frontier: The Impact of the Indian on American Culture." *In* Walker D. Wyman and Clifton B. Kroeber (eds.), *The Frontier in Perspective,* pp. 229–258. Madison: University of Wisconsin Press.

Harrington, John P.
1928 "Vocabulary of the Kiowa Language." *Bureau of American Ethnology, Bulletin* 84.

Harris, Marvin
1968 *The Rise of Anthropological Theory.* New York: Thomas Y. Crowell.

Hatton, O. Thomas
1974 "Performance Practices of Northern Plains Pow-Wow Singing Groups." Department of Music, Institute of Latin American Studies, University of Texas at Austin, *Yearbook,* pp. 123–137.

Hatton, Orin T.
1986 "In the Tradition: Grass Dance Musical Style and Female Pow-wow Singers." *Ethnomusicology* 30(2):197–222.

Helm, June (ed.)
1968 "Essays on the Problem of Tribe." *Proceedings of the American Ethnological Society.* (Available from University of Washington Press, Seattle.)

Heriard, Jack B.
1967– *Whispering Wind Magazine.* New Orleans.

Herskovits, Melville J.
1938 *Acculturation: The Study of Culture Contact.* New York: Augustin.

Hertzberg, Hazel W.
1971 *The Search for an American Indian Identity: Modern Pan-Indian Movements.* Syracuse, N.Y.: Syracuse University Press.

Herzog, George
1928 "Musical Styles in North America." *International Congress of Americanists, Proceedings* 23, pp. 455–458.

Hirabayashi, James, William Willard, and Luis Kemnitzer
1972 "Pan-Indianism in the Urban Setting." *In* Thomas Weaver and Douglas White (eds.), *The Anthropology of Urban Environments.* Society for Applied Anthropology, Monograph 11, pp. 77–87.

Hodge, William
1981 *The First Americans: Then and Now.* New York: Holt, Rinehart and Winston.
Howard, James H.
1951 "Notes on the Dakota Grass Dance." *Southwest Journal of Anthropology* 8:82–85.
1955 "The Pan-Indian Culture of Oklahoma." *The Scientific Monthly* 18(5):215–220.
1960 "Northern Style Grass Dance Costume." *American Indian Hobbyist* 7(1):18–27.
1965a "The Compleat Stomp Dancer." *Museum News, South Dakota Museum, Vermillion* Vol. 26, No. 5–6.
1965b "The Ponca Tribe." *Bureau of American Ethnology, Bulletin* 195.
1969 Record review of *War Dance Songs of the Ponca* (Indian House). *Ethnomusicology* 13 (1): 202–204.
1972a "Firecloud's Grass Dance or Omaha Costume, Part One." *American Indian Crafts and Culture* 6(2):2–9.
1972b "Firecloud's Omaha or Grass Dance Costume, Part Two." *American Indian Crafts and Culture* 6(3):2–8.
1976 "The Plains Gourd Dance as a Revitalization Movement." *American Ethnologist* 3(2):243–259.
1981 Review of W. Raymond Wood and Margot Liberty (1980).
1983 "Pan-Indianism in Native American Music and Dance." *Ethnomusicology* 27(1):71–82.
Hubbard, Ralph
1927 "Handicraft." In *Handbook for Boys,* pp. 538–547. New York: Boy Scouts of America.
Isaacs, Tony
1959 "Oklahoma Singing." *American Indian Hobbyist* 5(9–10):106–110.
James, Bernard
1961 "Social Psychological Dimensions of Ojibwa Acculturation." *American Anthropologist* (63):721–746.
Johnson, Michael G.
1972a "Canadian Santee and Plains Cree Grass Dance Costumes." *American Indian Crafts and Culture* 6(4):2–9.
1972b "The Clarence Dusty Horn Outfit. *American Indian Crafts and Culture* 6(9):2–5.
Johnston, James
1968a "Grass Dance Clothes." *Singing Wire* 2(3):5–10.
1968b "Grass Dance Clothes, Part 2." *Singing Wire* 2(4):7–9.
1968c "Grass Dance Clothes, Part 3." *Singing Wire* 2(5):10–12.

Johnston, Maureen, and James Johnston
    1968   "Modern Oklahoma Women's Costume." *Powwow Trails*
           5(3):28–30.
Josephy, Alvin M., Jr.
    1968   *The Indian Heritage of America*. New York: Bantam Books.
Kehoe, Alice B.
    1980   "The Giveaway Ceremony of Blackfoot and Plains Cree."
           Plains Anthropologist 25(87):17–26.
Kennedy, Michael Stephen
    1961   *The Assiniboines*, pp. 150–156. Norman: University of Okla-
           homa Press.
Koch, Ronald P.
    1977   *Dress Clothing of the Plains Indians*. Norman: University of
           Oklahoma Press.
Kroeber, A. L.
    1948   *Anthropology*, rev. ed. New York: Harcourt, Brace and World.
           (Original, 1923.)
Kurath, Gertrude P.
    1957   "Pan-Indianism in Great Lakes Tribal Festivals." *Journal of
           American Folklore* (70):179–182.
    1964   "Iroquois Music and Dance." *Bureau of American Ethnology,
           Bulletin* 187.
LaBarre, Weston
    1932   *The Peyote Cult*. New Haven: Yale University Press. (Revised
           1964.)
Laubin, Reginald, and Gladys Laubin
    1977   *Indian Dances of North America*. Norman: University of Okla-
           homa Press.
Leacock, Eleanor B., and Nancy O. Lurie (eds.)
    1971   *North American Indians in Historical Perspective*. New York:
           Random House.
Lessard, Rosemary
    1972   "Lakota Women's Dance Styles—a Brief Historical Survey."
           American Indian Crafts and Culture 6(4):15–17.
Lévi-Strauss, Claude
    1966   *The Savage Mind*. Chicago: University of Chicago Press. (Origi-
           nal, 1962.)
Levine, Stuart, and Nancy O. Lurie (eds.)
    1965   "The Indian Today." Special issue of *Midcontinent American
           Studies Journal* 6(2).
Linton, Ralph
    1943   "Nativistic Movements." *American Anthropologist* 45:230–
           239.

Lowie, Robert H.
1913 "Dance Associations of the Eastern Dakota." *American Museum of Natural History, Anthropological Papers* 11:102–142.
1914 "The Crow Sun Dance." *Journal of American Folklore* 28:94–96.
1915 "The Sun Dance of the Crow Indians." *American Museum of Natural History, Anthropological Papers* 16:1–50.
1916a "Plains Indian Age-Societies." *American Museum of Natural History, Anthropological Papers* 11(13):877–1031.
1916b "Societies of the Kiowa." *American Museum of Natural History, Anthropological Papers* 11(11):839–851.
1919 "Sun dance of the Shoshoni, Ute, and Hidatsa." *American Museum of Natural History, Anthropological Papers* 16(5):387–431.

Lurie, Nancy Oestreich
1965 "An American Indian Renascence?" *Midcontinent American Studies Journal* 6(2):25–50.
1971 "The Contemporary American Indian Scene." *In* Leacock and Lurie (eds.), pp. 418–480.

McAllester, David P.
1949 *Peyote Music.* New York: Viking Fund.
1968 "Navajo: Songs of the Dine. Record Review." *Ethnomusicology* 12(3):470–471.

Mason, Bernard S.
1944 *Dances and Stories of the American Indian.* New York: Ronald Press.

Mead, Margaret
1932 *Changing Culture of an Indian Tribe.* New York: Columbia University Press.

Merriam, Alan P.
1964 *The Anthropology of Music.* Evanston: Northwestern University Press.
1967 *Ethnomusicology of the Flathead Indians.* Chicago: Aldine.

Mishkin, Bernard
1940 *Rank and Warfare Among the Plains Indians.* Monographs of the American Ethnological Society, No. 3. Seattle: University of Washington Press.

Mooney, James
1896a "The Ghost-dance Religion and the Sioux Outbreak of 1890." *Bureau of American Ethnology, Annual Report* 14.
1896b "Calendar History of the Kiowa Indians." *Bureau of American Ethnology, 17th Annual Report,* pp. 141–147. Washington, DC.

1910 "Military Societies." *Handbook of the Indians North of Mexico.* Bureau of American Ethnology, *Bulletin* 30(1), pp. 861–863.

Moore, John H.
1974 "The Culture Concept as Ideology." *American Ethnologist* 1(3):537–549.

Morgan, Lawrence E.
1966– *Powwow Trails,* Vols. 4–6. South Plainfield, NJ.
1968

Murphy, Robert F.
1964 "Social Change and Acculturation." *Transactions of the New York Academy of Sciences* ser. 2, 26(7):845–854.

Nattiez, Jean-Jacques
1975 *Fondements d'une semiologie de la musique.* Paris: Union Générale d'Editions.

Nettl, Bruno
1954 *North American Indian Musical Styles.* Philadelphia: American Folklore Society.
1956 *Music in Primitive Culture.* Cambridge, MA: Harvard University Press.
1967a "Studies in Blackfoot Indian Musical Culture, Part I: Traditional Uses and Functions." *Ethnomusicology* 11(2):141–160.
1967b "Studies in Blackfoot Indian Musical Culture, Part II: Musical Life of the Montana Blackfoot, 1966." *Ethnomusicology* 11(3): 293–309.
1968a "Studies in Blackfoot Indian Musical Culture, Part III: Three Genres of Song." *Ethnomusicology* 12(1):11–48.
1968b "Studies in Blackfoot Indian Musical Culture, Part IV: Notes on Composition, Text, Settings and Performance." *Ethnomusicology* 12(2):192–207.

Newcomb, W. W., Jr.
1955 "A Note on Cherokee-Delaware Pan-Indianism." *American Anthropologist* (57):1041–1045.

Nurge, Ethel (ed.)
1970 *The Modern Sioux: Social Systems and Reservation Culture.* Lincoln: University of Nebraska Press.

Oswalt, Wendell H.
1978 *This Land Was Theirs: A Study of North American Indians,* 3rd ed. New York: John Wiley and Sons.

Owen, Roger C., James J. F. Deetz, and Anthony D. Fisher (eds.)
1967 *The North American Indians: A Sourcebook.* New York: Macmillan.

Petrullo, Vincenzo
  1934   *The Diabolic Root: A Study of Peyotism.* Philadelphia: University
         of Pennsylvania Press.
Powers, Marla N.
  1986   *Oglala Women in Myth, Ritual and Reality.* Chicago: University
         of Chicago Press.
  1988   "Symbolic Representations of Sex Roles in the Plains War
         Dance." *European Review of Native American Studies* 2(2):17–
         24.
Powers, William K.
  1961a "The Sioux Omaha Dance." *American Indian Tradition* 8(1):
         24–33.
  1961b "American Indian Music: Contemporary Music and Dance of
         the Western Sioux." *American Indian Tradition* 7(5):158–165.
  1962a "The Rabbit Dance." *American Indian Tradition* 8(3):113–118.
  1962b "Sneak-up Dance, Drum Dance, and Flag Dance." *American
         Indian Tradition* 8(4):166–171.
  1964– *Powwow Trails,* Vols. 1–3. Somerset, NJ.
  1966
  1966a *Here Is Your Hobby: Indian Dancing and Costumes.* New York:
         Putnam's.
  1966b "Feathers Costume." *Powwow Trails* 3(7–8):4–14, 19.
  1967   "Okan: Sun Dance of the Blackfoot. Film Review." *American
         Anthropologist* 69(5):561–562.
  1968   "Contemporary Oglala Music and Dance: Pan-Indianism Ver-
         sus Pan-Tetonism." *Ethnomusicology* 12(3):352–372.
  1969   *Indians of the Northern Plains.* New York: G. P. Putnam's Sons.
  1971   *Indians of the Southern Plains.* New York: G. P. Putnam's Sons.
  1977   *Oglala Religion.* Lincoln: University of Nebraska Press.
  1980a "Plains Indian Music and Dance." *In* W. Raymond Wood and
         Margot Liberty, eds., *Anthropology on the Great Plains.* Lincoln:
         University of Nebraska Press.
  1980b "Oglala Song Terminology." In *Selected Reports in Ethnomusi-
         cology,* Vol. III, No. 2, Charlotte Heth, ed., pp. 23–42. Los
         Angeles: University of California Press.
  1982   *Yuwipi: Vision and Experience in Oglala Ritual.* Lincoln: Univer-
         sity of Nebraska Press.
  1986   *Sacred Language: The Nature of Supernatural Discourse in Lakota.*
         Norman: University of Oklahoma Press.
  1987   *Beyond the Vision: Essays on American Indian Culture.* Norman:
         University of Oklahoma Press.
  1988a "The Indian Hobbyist Movement." *In* Wilcomb E. Washburn

(ed.), *Indian-White Relations*. Vol. 4 of *Handbook of North American Indians*. Washington, DC: Smithsonian Institution.

1988b "Foolish Words: Text and Context in Lakota Love Songs." *European Review of Native American Studies* 2(2): 29–34.

———— and Marla N. Powers

1984 "Metaphysical Aspects of an Oglala Food System." *In* Mary Douglas (ed.), *Food in the Social Order*. New York: Russell Sage Foundation.

Price, John A.

1968 "The Migration and Adaptation of American Indians to Los Angeles." *Human Organization* (27):168–175.

1978 *Native Studies: American and Canadian Indians*. Toronto: McGraw-Hill Ryerson.

Prucha, Francis Paul (ed.)

1971 *The Indian in American History*. Hinsdale, IL: Dryden Press.

1977 *A Bibliographical Guide to the History of Indian-White Relations in the United States*. Chicago: University of Chicago Press.

Rachlin, Carol K.

1964 "The Native American Church in Oklahoma." *Chronicles of Oklahoma* (42):262–272.

1965 "Tight Shoe Night." *Midcontinent American Studies Journal* 6(2):84–100.

Redfield, Robert, Ralph Linton, and Melville Herskovits.

1936 "Memorandum for the Study of Acculturation." *American Anthropologist* (38):149–152. (Reprinted in Bohannan and Plog 1967.)

Rhoades, Sandy

1970 "The Bugler in the Taip-iah Gourd Dance Society." *American Indian Crafts and Culture* 4(7):12.

Rhodes, Willard

1960 "The Christian Hymnology of the North American Indians." In *Men and Cultures: Selected Papers of the Fifth International Congress of Anthropological and Ethnological Sciences, 1956*. Philadelphia: University of Pennsylvania Press.

1963 "North American Indian Music in Transition." *Journal of the International Folk Music Council* 15:9–14.

1967 "Acculturation in North American Indian Music." *In* Sol Tax, ed., *Acculturation in the Americas*, pp. 127–132. New York: Cooper Square Publishers.

Roberts, Helen H.

1936 "Musical Areas in Aboriginal North America." *Yale University Publications in Anthropology* 12.

Salomon, Julian H.
   1928   *The Book of Indian Crafts and Indian Lore.* New York: Harper
           and Brothers.
Sanford, Margaret
   1971   "Pan-Indianism, Acculturation and the American Ideal."
           Plains Anthropologist 16(53):222–227.
Schusky, Ernest
   1957   "Pan-Indianism in the Eastern United States." *Anthropology
           Tomorrow* (6):116–123.
Seton, Ernest T.
   1927   *The Birch Bark Roll.* N.p.: Ernest Thompson Seton.
Sheehy, Daniel
   1979   Review of *Indian Music of Northwest Mexico. Ethnomusicology*
           23(2):352–354.
Skinner, Alanson
   1919a   "The Sun Dance of the Plains Ojibwa." *American Museum of
           Natural History, Anthropological Papers* 16(4):311–315.
   1919b   "The Sun Dance of the Plains Cree." *American Museum of
           Natural History, Anthropological Papers* 16(4):283–293.
   1919c   "Notes on the Sun Dance of the Sisseton Dakota." *American
           Museum of Natural History, Anthropological Papers* 16(4):381–
           385.
Slotkin, J. S.
   1956   *The Peyote Religion. A Study in Indian-White Relations.* Glencoe,
           IL: The Free Press.
Smith, Jerry, and Randy Kroha
   1972   "Oklahoma Feather Dancers." *American Indian Crafts and Cul-
           ture* 6(5): 2–7.
Spencer, Robert F., Jesse D. Jennings, et al.
   1977   *The Native Americans,* 2nd ed. New York: Harper and Row.
Spier, Leslie
   1921a   "The Sun Dance of the Plains Indians." *American Museum of
           Natural History, Anthropological Papers* 16(6):451–527.
   1921b   "Notes on the Kiowa Sun Dance." *American Museum of Natu-
           ral History, Anthropological Papers* 16(6):433–450.
Stewart, Omer C.
   1980   "The Native American Church." *In* Raymond Wood and Mar-
           got Liberty (eds.), *Anthropology on the Great Plains.* Lincoln:
           University of Nebraska Press.
Stewart, Tyrone H.
   1967–   *American Indian Crafts and Culture.* Tulsa, OK.
   1974

1970   "Southern Style Cloth Dress." *American Indian Crafts and Culture* 4(8):2–5, 13.

——— and Jerry Smith

1973   *The Oklahoma Feather Dancer.* Tulsa, OK: American Indian Crafts and Culture.

Tax, Sol (ed.)

1967   *Acculturation in the Americas.* New York: Cooper Square Publishers.

Theisz, R. D.

1974   "The Contemporary 'Traditional Style' of the Lakota." *American Indian Crafts and Culture* 8(6):2–7.

1981   "Acclamations and Accolades: Honor Songs in Lakota Society Today." *The Kansas Quarterly* 13(2): 27–43.

Thomas, Robert K.

1965   "Pan-Indianism." *Midcontinent American Studies Journal* 6(2): 75–83.

Thornton, J. Gordon

1964   *Kiowa.* Ethnic Folkways Record No. FE 4393.

Tucker, M. S.

1969   *Old Time Sioux Dancers.* Tulsa: American Indian Crafts and Culture.

Turley, Frank

1966   "Dance Revivals." *Powwow Trails* 2(9):7.

Van Gennep, Arnold

1960   *The Rites of Passage.* Chicago: University of Chicago Press. (Original, 1909.)

Voget, Fred W.

1956   "The American Indian in Transition: Reformation and Accommodation." *American Anthropologist* 58(2):249–263.

Vogt, Evon Z.

1967   "The Acculturation of American Indians." In Roger C. Owen, J. J. F. Deetz, and A. D. Fisher (eds.), *The North American Indians,* pp. 636–647. New York: Macmillan. (Original, 1957.)

Walker, J. R.

1917   "The Sun Dance and Other Ceremonies of the Oglala Division of the Teton Dakota." *American Museum of Natural History, Anthropological Papers* 16(2):51–221.

Wallace, Anthony F. C.

1956   "Revitalization Movements." *American Anthropologist* 58: 264–281.

1966   *Religion: An Anthropological View.* New York: Random House.

Wallis, W. D.
1919 "The Sun Dance of the Canadian Dakota." *American Museum of Natural History, Anthropological Papers* 16(2):317–380.

Ward, John
1969 "Northern Style Powwow." *Singing Wire* 3(2):9–10.
1970a "Modern Crow Men's Dance Outfit." *American Indian Crafts and Culture* 4(2):2–6.
1970b "Modern Crow Men's Dance Outfit, Part 2." *American Indian Crafts and Culture* 4(4):2–5.
1970c "Modern Crow Men's Dance Outfit, Part 3." *American Indian Crafts and Culture* 4(5):2–7.

Wax, Murray L., and Robert W. Buchanan (eds.)
1975 *Solving "The Indian Problem": The White Man's Burdensome Business.* New York: Franklin Watts.

Weist, Katherine M.
1973 "Giving Away: The Ceremonial Distribution of Goods Among the Northern Cheyenne of Southeastern Montana." *Plains Anthropologist* 18(60):97–103.

White, Leslie
1959 *The Evolution of Culture.* New York: McGraw-Hill.

Wissler, Clark
1912 "Societies and Ceremonial Associations in the Oglala Division of the Teton Dakota." *American Museum of Natural History, Anthropological Papers* 11(1):1–99.
1916 "General Discussion of Shamanistic and Dancing Societies." *American Museum of Natural History, Anthropological Papers* 11(12):853–876.
1918 "The Sun Dance of the Blackfoot Indians." *American Museum of Natural History, Anthropological Papers* 16(3):223–270.

Wood, Raymond, and Margot Liberty (eds.)
1980 *Anthropology on the Great Plains.* Lincoln: University of Nebraska Press.

Index

ABOUT THE AUTHOR

WILLIAM K. POWERS is Professor of Anthropology at Rutgers University and Director of the Graduate Certificate Program in North American Indian Studies, which he founded there in 1986.

He received the Ph.D. in anthropology from the University of Pennsylvania and has spent over 40 years researching American Indian music, dance, and religion. The author of 12 books and over 200 articles on American Indian culture, he also writes plays, poetry, and music.